When evangelicals care

— the story of
Pilgrims' Friend Society

PILGRIMS'
FRIEND
SOCIETY

Brian H Edwards

DayOne

© Day One Publications 2017

ISBN 978-1-84625-566-3

All Scripture quotations, unless stated otherwise, are from The Holy Bible, New International Version Copyright © 1973, 1978, 1984 International Bible Society

British Library Cataloguing in Publication Data available

Published by Day One Publications
Ryelands Road, Leominster, HR6 8NZ
Telephone 01568 613 740   Fax 01568 611 473
North America Toll Free 888 329 6630
email—sales@dayone.co.uk
web site—www.dayone.co.uk

Cover design by smallprint

Cover images:
Top—Part of the first home of the Aged Pilgrims' Friend Society at Camberwell
Bottom—Pilgrim Gardens, Evington, Leicestershire (© Tim Crocker)

Printed by Orchard Press Ltd Cheltenham

Contents

'The path of the righteous is like the first gleam of dawn, shining ever brighter till the full light of day'
Proverbs 4:18

By contrast:

'When service should in my old limbs lie lame and unregarded age in corners thrown.'
Shakespeare, *As You Like It*, Act 2, Scene 3

Foreword

I t is a great privilege to be involved with an organisation that has a
fresh and exciting sense of God's calling for its third century.

The story of the Pilgrims' Friend Society will be of interest not only to all
who support the charity, but also to those who want to understand the role
played by evangelical Christians in alleviating much of the suffering in 19th
century London. Beyond this, it may also be helpful to other organisations
that, like the Pilgrims' Friend Society, want to remain unswervingly true
to their central purpose and the Christian gospel and yet need to change
the way that they work for it to be effective in a rapidly changing world.

The story that Brian Edwards tells is of a group of young Christians who
took Scripture seriously and dared to love and care for those neglected by
others—the 'aged pilgrims' whose condition was desperate even by the
standards of the day. They did so despite little initial support and even
direct opposition from many in the established churches.

The unfolding record shows how the Society has stayed true to its
mission and its evangelical basis even though it has had to work its way
through some very profound changes in how it operates: from a pensions
fund to a residential care provider, from a faith mission to charging fees,
from caring only for Christians to offering its services to a wider public,
and finally to respond to today's challenges of care increasingly being
delivered within the community.

The story also reveals a charity with a persistent and sustained biblical
focus on the people it was set up to serve, seen through the eyes and heart
of the Lord Jesus. Preaching on behalf of the charity on 24 March 1839,

James Evans summed up the purpose of the mission: 'I plead not for them (the destitute elderly) but for the cause of Christ.' Perhaps this is how the charity has managed change without succumbing to the twin dangers of inflexible dogma and liberal flexibility.

In producing this account, the trustees pray that it will encourage evangelical Christians to take the lead again in engaging with older people, because without this many will face an unfruitful older age, decline and death without the hope and comfort offered by the Christian faith.

The Christian church is surely the best equipped to help society rediscover in the 21st century what the pioneers of Pilgrims' Friend Society knew: the value of elderly people and that there are ways of living in older age, with degrees of dependency, that are dignified and purposeful—and we all have a role to play in this.

Stephen Hammersley
Chief Executive
London 2017

*The new award-winning Pilgrim Garden complex in Evington,
Leicestershire opened in 2014 (© Tim Crocker)*

Slums of London, an engraving by Gustave Dore, c. 1850

1. 'The worst of times'

When Victoria came to the throne in June 1837 she was soon to rule over an empire 'on which the sun never sets'. It was the largest empire the world had ever known, extended and defended by the seemingly invincible 'thin red line' of British regiments. The massacres abroad to grasp the wealth of nations were matched by misery at home to support it. Vast wealth poured into the country from the overseas 'acquisitions' and this, along with the advent of steamships and the railways, electricity and telegraphy, fed the industrial revolution that saw a massive growth in cities. Over the first fifty years of the century the population of Manchester grew from 84,000 to 303,000, and during the same period the one million population of London doubled.

Human nature being what it is, tragically and inevitably, all the massive increase in wealth and the advance in technology did almost nothing for the multitude of labouring poor who were squeezed into ghettos of poverty. It was little better in rural England. In 1847 a Suffolk labourer commented,

'These mushroom great people have all grown up since I remember, and if I speak to them of the hard times, they tell me to look at the great improvements, the new docks, the cheap postage, the fine railways; really, say they, this is a grand and glorious country; Sir Robert hath repealed the Corn Laws and Lord John will drain our streets and erect baths. Oh! What a blessed land this is. Well, say I, very good, but what benefit has it conferred on me? Here I am working harder than ever, poorer than ever, with no remedy for want and no hope but death. The railway whizzes past my door, but I never had my foot in a railway carriage. I have no correspondence but with my neighbours … my brown bread is dearer, my wages are no higher. The great docks with their many ships, the great railways and fast-running mail carts, have added not a stone to my cottage, nor a crumb to my table.'

In the great cities, the resulting massive overcrowding led to slums that were filthy, unhealthy and violent. Charles Dickens aptly described

Chapter 1

London and Paris at the end of the previous century: 'It was the best of times; it was the worst of times' (*A Tale of Two Cities*, 1859).

To step back into 19th century London—vividly although only partially portrayed by Dickens—is to step into a world so at variance with our modern western society as to be almost unbelievable. 'The submerged tenth' of the population, as William Booth the founder of the Salvation Army described it, lived in hopeless poverty. Whole families were crammed into miserable slums with few possessions and often no income. The state of the lodging houses was no better, with twenty or thirty people living in a room fit only for three. And for this they paid exorbitant rents. An estimated 80,000 occupied these lodging houses in London.

When, in September 1841, Lord Shaftesbury toured Whitechapel and Bethnal Green 'to see with my own eyes the suffering and degradation which unwholesome residences inflict on the poorer classes', he concluded graphically: 'No pen or paintbrush could describe the thing as it is. One whiff of Cowyard, Blue Anchor, or Bakers' Court, outweighs ten pages of letterpress.'[1]

At the beginning of the century the slums of London, known as 'rookeries' because of their overcrowding, were some of the worst. Of the one million people, and rising rapidly, who lived in London, 134,000 of them were crammed within the square mile of the City itself. It is not hard to imagine the results of sleeping seventeen people in a single room without sanitation. One of the most notorious slum areas was Locks Field, just off the fashionable New Kent Road, but Old Westminster and Tothill Fields were as bad, and the local names revealed the lives of those who lived there: Rogue's Acre, Dirty Lane, Long Ditch, Pickpocket's Alley, Bandy Leg Walk.

Men lolled idly, dirty and dishevelled, hoping for a day's employment. Without employment they had little option but to join the buffers, smashers, nosers, sharpers, bustlers and pick-pockets to earn their living another way. Robbery invaded all corners of London life; every crowd

1 Edwin Hodder, *The Life and Work of the Seventh Earl of Shaftesbury* (London: Cassell and Company Limited, 1892), p. 196.

was infested with pick-pockets, just as almost everyone's hair was infested with lice. Inevitably rioting and fighting—the latter particularly popular when women were involved—were commonplace and at times it required up to fifty constables with cutlasses to deal with trouble.

The streets of the slums were narrow and often unpaved; although gas lamps on some streets were introduced in 1807, few had any light at all after midnight since the lamp-lighters frequently sold a proportion of their oil. Lord Vice owned the slums, and Filth and Lice were tenants. With more than six thousand cheap gin shops in London, drink dried up tears and burned up hearts so that thousands seemed to live and die without a soul. In the district of Euston Road there was one public house to every hundred people—counting men, women and children; and in Orange Street, Leicester Square, there were one hundred gin-palaces, 'most of them very large'.

The Great Stink

Although the Fleet Ditch had been covered over in the middle of the previous century, there were still no effective sewers in London when Victoria promised 'to be good' on her accession to the throne. All imaginable and unimaginable filth and excrement was tipped onto the streets in the hope that the rain would wash it away. The stench on a warm summer afternoon was unbearable. London was built upon overflowing and stinking cesspits—often only feet away from the wells from which the population obtained their drinking water; the open sewers in the middle of the streets were generally blocked and consequently foul. In 1850 the curtains in Parliament and better-off homes were soaked in chloride of lime to mask the smell of what was dubbed 'The Great Stink' from the slow-moving sewage of the Thames. It was another four years before the young physician, John Snow, linked cholera with the foul water people were drinking. Cholera, typhoid, dysentery and smallpox were rife, though tuberculosis (consumption) was still the major killer.

The most vulnerable in this society were the sick and disabled, the children and the elderly.

Chapter 1

The sick and disabled

Attention had been drawn to the plight of the blind and the deaf back in the 18th century, but it was left to evangelical Christians to put some of the ideas into practice. By the mid-19th-century it was estimated there were 30,000 blind people in Britain, mostly in the cities and large towns. In 1868 Dr Thomas Armitage became the founder of what later was known as the Royal National Institute for the Blind. However, in 1843 the Christian Blind Relief Society was the first society to grant pensions to blind people irrespective of age. It took another eighty years before the state granted a pension to blind people at the age of 50.

The picture was similar for those who were deaf, and for the mentally ill. The work of the evangelical Congregational minister, Andrew Reed, among those with learning disabilities, was far ahead of his time. Opening his first home at Highgate in 1848 he modelled an enlightened Christian care for such people.

Andrew Reed is little known today, but in the 19th century the pastor of New Road Chapel in Stepney (later rebuilt and renamed Wycliffe Chapel) was widely known for his vital work in establishing three orphanages, two homes for those with what we call today 'learning disabilities', and a 'hospice' for those with severe physical disabilities. Andrew Reed's two asylums for 'idiots'—not then a pejorative term but a recognised medical description—ventured into the complex world of caring for adults with learning disabilities. His was an age when such people were either totally ignored, locked away, or became the object of amusement for the general public. Reed and his workers established a home with a modern-day wisdom and insight: not a rigid, soul-destroying institution, but a happy, loving, active and progressive family. It was all quite remarkable for any day, but most of all for the 19th century.

Misunderstood by friends, ridiculed by opponents, betrayed by those he trusted, and hampered by narrow-minded bigotry, Andrew Reed was a giant in faith and self-discipline who passionately believed that *every* individual had value simply because they had been created in the image of God—and that nothing would be impossible if he reached out for the hand of God.[2]

Until the Idiots Act of 1886 Andrew Reed's homes were the only asylums where those with learning disabilities could be educated and equipped with a skill for life. His later career for those with incurable disabilities led eventually to the Hospital for Incurables in Wandsworth in 1863.[3]

The newly built Bethlem (Bedlam) Hospital at St George's Fields, which opened in 1815, hardly improved on the atrocious care of those with mental disabilities, known as lunatics or idiots. Once again, it was left to the Christians, and in particular the Quaker Edward Wakefield, to alert the nation to the terrible abuses.

The children

Inevitably, infant deaths were tragically high, especially in the overcrowded and insanitary London. Reliable figures are available for the mortality of children in the first three decades of the 19th century. One third of all children died before reaching the age of five years[4]— compared with 0.5% today. This was at least an improvement on a century earlier when three quarters of all children died before that age— Queen Anne bore seventeen children, only one survived infancy and he died at the age of eleven years.

It is this alarming figure of Victorian infant mortality that skews most statistics on expected life spans at birth in the 19th century, which was not much above twenty-two years for a labourer living in the slums. In reality, if he could survive the first five years of childhood he might add another twenty years to that average. However, as late as the end of the century attempts to recruit fit young men for the campaign against the Boers in South Africa revealed that only two in nine working-class men from

2   Ian J Shaw, *Andrew Reed—The Greatest is Charity* (Darlington: Evangelical Press, 2005).
3   The hospital still occupies these, now listed, buildings. In 1917 the name changed to the Royal Hospital and Home for Incurables, and in 1988 to the Royal Hospital and Home. It is now The Royal Hospital for Neuro-disability and is a world leader in care for those with brain injuries.
4   R. M. Rayner, *Nineteenth Century England* (London: Longmans, Green and Co., 1927). p. 142.

London were sufficiently fit to be enlisted. For those in Victorian England who did survive their fifth birthday, life among the poor was not far short of a living death.

It was no better in the industrial heartland of the North where women and children worked fourteen or fifteen hours a day in the mines and factories, and where children as young as five and six years old were mutilated in the mills or crushed by the coal trucks underground. At the same time, an estimated 30,000 'naked, filthy, roaming, lawless and deserted children' lived on the streets of Dickens' London. These were children of 'whores, pick-pockets, footpads, housebreakers, and thieves of every description.' They lived by their wits and slept where they could; if they stole they ate, and if they didn't they starved.

Slum children of whom an estimated 30,000 lived homeless and lawless on the streets of Victorian London

Addressing the London Society for the Improvement of the Conditions of Factory Children, Lord Shaftesbury claimed that those who once sacrificed their children to the god Moloch and the Indians who killed their unwanted babies: 'were a merciful people compared with Englishmen in the 19th century ... For those nations destroyed at once their wretched offspring, and prevented a long career of suffering and crime; but we, having sucked out every energy of body and of soul, toss them on the world a mass of skin and bone, incapable of exertion, brutalised in their understanding, and disqualified for immortality.'[5]

Chimney sweeps, known as climbing boys, from four years old and upwards, many stolen or sold, were forced up the chimneys of the wealthy, often accompanied by blows or lighted wisps of straw. Many suffocated in the choking labyrinth and all suffered respiratory diseases and terrible skin cancers; this did not end until 1840. Hundreds of orphaned children simply looked after one another. An investigation discovered in a room in one house nine motherless children. The mother's death was caused by witnessing one of her children being run over. The eldest child was only fourteen years old. All lived in one small room, and there was only one bed for five. This was not uncommon.

By the time of his death in 1862, Andrew Reed—described in his day simply as 'The orphans' friend'—had provided homes for 6,400 children and adults from among the forgotten of society. In his homes the children were cared for in a family atmosphere, were well fed and educated, and provided with a box under their bed for their personal possessions. Reed founded The London Orphan Society in 1813, more than two decades before George Müller opened his orphanage in Bristol, and half a century before the Baptist pastor C H Spurgeon and Dr Thomas Barnardo opened theirs in London. In the year of her accession to the throne, Queen Victoria became a patron of Andrew Reed's orphanage.

The elderly

As with the sick and disabled, virtually nothing was provided for the elderly. From early in the 17th century it had been the duty of Poor Law authorities to care for the elderly, but such care was generally to be found only in the many trusts of previous centuries. However, the continual move away from rural communities, where the extended family generally cared for their elderly relatives, meant that the destitute elderly became

---

5 Edwin Hodder, *The Life and Work of the Seventh Earl of Shaftesbury* (London: Cassell and Company Limited, 1892), p. 84.

lost in the cities. In the chaos of London slums it was impossible for the state to identify those in need; besides, there was no provision for them anyway. The National Assistance Act of 1948, when local authorities were obliged to provide homes for the elderly, lay a long way ahead.

Victorian poor elderly women

Charitable almshouses did exist, but they were pitifully few to care for the growing number of the men and women too frail to work and with no family wishing or able to support them. Even for the elderly, beyond begging, the only resort was the dreaded workhouse. It was certainly in the thinking of Victorian England that those who would not work, would not eat. Therefore, the little help that was occasionally available for the sick was intended only to get them back to work. What was unintentionally, or conveniently, overlooked was the fact that there were many who through age and infirmity, could not work.

Nowhere was Shakespeare's 16th century reference to 'unregarded age in corners thrown'[6] more evidenced than in 19th century London.

The founders of the Aged Pilgrims' Friend Society lamented that 'one numerous class of deserving persons is left deserted and forsaken, namely, the aged and infirm Christian poor'. They went on to describe the condition of many:

'Who, after having spent a laborious life in poverty, and worn out with old age and bodily infirmity are, in the winter of life, shut up in garrets and cellars lingering the remainder of their days in distress and wretchedness, deserted by the world ... and neglected by those of the same household of faith of which they are members ...

6   Shakespeare, *As You Like It*, Adam to Orlando in Act 2, Scene 3.

Some of these dear aged Pilgrims have been found so distressed as to be almost starving with hunger, and destitute of clothing or any bed to rest their infirm limbs except a little straw on the floor, and without any covering but what few rags they had on afforded them.'[7]

The Bitter Cry...

In these, and all areas of desperate social need, things only improved slightly towards the end of the 19th century. But when the century opened, what social care there was came largely from individuals and their supporters; the Christian denominations, and even local churches, were not significantly involved. This fact was lamented by the pamphlet *The Bitter Cry of Outcast London—an enquiry into the condition of the abject poor*, published by the Rev. Andrew Wearns of the London Congregational Union in October 1883.[8] It was the result of 'a long, sober and patient enquiry undertaken for the purpose

THE BITTER CRY

OF

OUTCAST LONDON.

AN INQUIRY INTO THE CONDITION OF THE ABJECT POOR.

THERE is no more hopeful sign in the Christian Church of to-day than the increased attention which is being given by it to the poor and outcast classes of society. Of these it has never been wholly neglectful; if it had it would have ceased to be Christian. But it has, as yet, only imperfectly realised and fulfilled its mission to the poor. Until recently it has contented itself with sustaining some outside organisations, which have charged themselves with this special function, or what is worse, has left the matter to individuals or to little bands of Christians having no organisation. For the rest it has been satisfied with a superficial and inadequate district visitation, with the more or less indiscriminate distribution of material charities, and with opening a few rooms here and there into which the poorer people have been gathered, and by which a few have been rescued. All this is good in its way and has done good; but by all only the merest edge of the great dark region of poverty, misery, squalor and immorality has been touched. We are not losing sight of the London City Mission, whose agents are everywhere, and whose noble work our investigations have led us to value more than ever, but after all has been done the churches are making the discovery that seething in the very centre of our great cities, concealed by the thinnest crust of civilization and decency, is a vast mass of moral corruption, of heart-breaking misery and absolute godless-

A

rice One Penny; or Six Shillings per 100.

The first page of 'The Bitter Cry' which was so influential in raising an awareness of London poverty in 1883

---

7 From the foundation document of the Aged Pilgrims' Friend Society, 1807.
8 First published anonymously, *The Bitter Cry of Outcast London—an enquiry into the condition of the abject poor*, Rev. Andrew Wearn (Fleet Street, London: James Clarke & Co., October 1883).

of discovering the actual state of the case and the remedial action most likely to be effective'. London was 'a vast mass of moral corruption, of heart-breaking misery and absolute godlessness'. The pamphlet regretted the fact that social care had been left by the churches 'to individuals or to little bands of Christians having no organisation'. It continued:

'It is easy to bring an array of facts which seem to point to the opposite conclusion—to speak of the noble army of men and women who penetrate the vilest haunts, carrying with them the blessings of the gospel; of the encouraging reports published by Missions, Reformatories, Refuges, Temperance Societies; of Theatre Services, Midnight Meetings and Special Missions. But what does it all amount to? We are simply living in a fool's paradise if we suppose that all these agencies combined are doing a thousandth part of what needs to be done, a hundredth part of what could be done by the Church of Christ.'

The Bitter Cry shocked a 'Christian' nation with its stark description of the London slums:

'In one cellar a sanitary inspector reports finding a father, mother, three children, and four pigs! In another room a missionary found a man ill with small-pox, his wife just recovering from her eighth confinement, and the children running about half naked and covered with dirt. Here are seven people living in one underground kitchen, and a little dead child lying in the same room. Elsewhere is a poor widow, her three children, and a child who had been dead thirteen days. Her husband, who was a cabman, had shortly before committed suicide. Here lives a widow and her six children, including one daughter of 29, another of 21, and a son of 27. Another apartment contains father, mother, and six children, two of whom are ill with scarlet fever. In another nine brothers and sisters, from 29 years of age downwards, live, eat and sleep together. Here is a mother who turns her children into the street in the early evening because she lets her room for immoral purposes until long after midnight, when the poor little wretches creep back again if they have not found some miserable shelter elsewhere....'

And so it continued—a description worse than Dickens and almost beyond imagination.

Charitable work was undertaken mainly by individuals who formed societies outside of the churches. This was true of both the established church and the nonconformists. Even the Quakers were at first concerned almost exclusively for their own people. The appeal of *The Bitter Cry* was that 'a combined and organised effort' needed to be made by the denominations working together.

By the middle of the 19th century the crusade to lift the poor out of poverty gathered momentum. In Parliament Lord Ashley—on his father's death in 1851 he became the seventh Earl of Shaftesbury—was struggling to reduce the hours that women and girls would be allowed to work in factories, to improve the working conditions of children, chimney sweep boys, factory workers, those in asylums and a host more. But largely he was alone. He complained that he received almost no support from those of influence in the church or the state: 'I am like a pelican in the wilderness or a sparrow on the housetops. I have no one with whom I can take counsel, no one to aid me, no one to cheer me.' Shaftesbury despaired of help from what he called 'the evangelical religionists'. Andrew Reed in his farsighted work to care for those with learning disabilities found exactly the same. Not until Albert, the Prince Consort, supported him did Reed suddenly find clergymen interested in his cause.

Twelve months after Victoria ascended the throne, a popular movement sent ripples of fear among the wealthy. During its brief history, the movement was known as Chartism when millions of workers across the country campaigned, by means of mass meetings and petitions, for a free vote for all men and an end to the corruption of the current political system.

The aristocracy had good reason to be anxious, because Europe was convulsed in revolutions by the working people. In response to the fear of the rising power of the workers Lord Shaftesbury wrote in his diary for 21 July 1848—a significant year of revolution across Europe: 'Talk of the dangerous classes, indeed! The dangerous classes in England are not the people! The dangerous classes are the lazy ecclesiastics, of whom there are thousands, and the rich who do no good with their money! I fear them more than whole battalions of chartists.'[9]

In that year, even the Queen and the Prince Consort were concerned for the poor, which was understandable with revolution 'going off like pop guns' in Italy, Austria and France.

The non-conformist voice

The main assault on the cruel poverty came from nonconformist evangelicals (also known as 'dissenters'). They covered virtually every area of need but had, at least early in the century, little voice, especially because they were held in low regard by the establishment both in society and the church. Even Shaftesbury admitted that he had been brought up in the old 'high and dry' school of religion where it was considered a matter of merit to hate dissenters. He complained, although with some exaggeration, that only Bishop Stanley of Norwich would be seen on the platform with dissenters.

Until the repeal of the Test and Corporation Act in 1828, it was not possible for dissenters to enter Parliament or serve on a local council unless they could sign the Thirty-nine Articles of the Church of England, nor could they take a degree at the universities of Oxford and Cambridge. They could not be buried in an Anglican churchyard by a nonconformist minister, and marriages in nonconformist chapels were not legally recognised. Until the Registration of Births, Deaths and Marriages Act of 1836, dissenters frequently could not even prove their age, and until the Solemnisation of Marriages Acts in the same year there were no civil marriages and for many Anglicans, dissenters were not legally married and therefore 'lived in sin'. In 1843 Andrew Reed felt compelled to resign from the Infant Orphan Asylum, which he had founded and steered for thirteen years, because the Anglicans on his committee demanded that even the very young children must be taught the Church of England

9   Edwin Hodder, *The Life and Work of the Seventh Earl of Shaftesbury* (London: Cassell and Company Limited, 1892), p. 402.

catechism; Reed's non-sectarian plea was ignored. A year later he sadly resigned from the London Orphan Society for the same reason.[10]

Accurate statistics are hard to gain for charitable work in the Victorian period, but one detailed researcher concludes, 'It does appear that as many as three quarters of the total number of charitable organisations in the second half of the 19th century can be regarded as evangelical in character and control.'[11] This assessment is confirmed by Shaftesbury's own in 1884, the year before his death: 'I am essentially and from deep-rooted conviction an Evangelical of the Evangelicals. I have worked with them constantly, and I am satisfied that most of the great philanthropic movements of the century have sprung from them....'[12] In both instances, it was the evangelical nonconformists who were principally in mind.

We may be critical of the Victorians—for their arrogance, mistakes and failures—but unlike our contemporary and contemptuous society, the many evangelical organisations that were formed to help the destitute were free to do their work in the open context of caring for the eternal welfare of those in need. The connection between the Christian gospel and the motivation of their work was recognised by all, and few complained.

Evangelicals were at the forefront of charitable work—and still are—because they saw every human being not as a highly developed anthropoid, but as an individual person created in the image of God. The elderly widow suffering her arthritic pain without fire or food, the drunken father lying stupidly in his vomit, the young pregnant prostitute plying the ill-lit back streets of London, the weeping mother with her starving brood of half-clothed children, and the destitute child shivering in a box under a railway arch, were each created by God and for God, and needed to be rescued from their appalling suffering and reconnected to their Creator through the gospel of Jesus Christ. That was the motivation of the greatest amount of charitable work in London and the cities—and, unashamedly, evangelical Christians were at the

10 Ian J Shaw, *Andrew Reed—The Greatest is Charity*, pp. 194-199.
11 Kathleen Heasman, *Evangelicals in Action* (London: Geoffrey Bles., 1962). Her PhD thesis, p. 14.
12 Edwin Hodder, *The Life and Work of the Seventh Earl of Shaftesbury* (London: Cassell and Company Limited, 1892), p. 519.

forefront. As with all his concern for humanity, Shaftesbury commented, 'I must regard the objects of it as beings created, as ourselves, by the same Maker, redeemed by the same Saviour, and determined to the same immortality.'

It was this conviction, that every individual is of value because created in the image of God, that motivated not only Shaftesbury and Andrew Reed, but the thousands of evangelical Christians who either initiated or supported charities to aid the disadvantaged in society: the Indigent Blind Visiting Society, Holloway Ragged School, the Cripples' Home, St Giles Prison Mission, the Cabmen's Shelter Fund, Stockwell Orphanages, the British Asylum for Deaf and Dumb, Discharged Prisoners' Aid Society, National Cripple Boys' Home, Homes for Inebriates, Infant Orphan Asylum, Female Mission to the Fallen, and literally scores more.

In January 1861 Lord Shaftesbury had urged the Bristol YMCA: 'Christianity is not a state of opinion and speculation. Christianity is essentially practical... Therefore, I say to you again and again, let your Christianity be practical.' More than two decades later, in July 1885 at the age of 84, he was still as busy as ever with Parliamentary and charitable business, and in this, his last year, he took up the cause of child prostitution. By the early autumn he travelled to Folkestone for a brief rest; careless as ever for himself, he caught a chill and pneumonia set in. Shaftesbury, known by himself and many as 'Lord of the great unwashed', died peacefully in the afternoon of 1 October 1885.

Although he had been offered Westminster Abbey, Shaftesbury requested a simple burial at St Giles on his home estate in Dorset. His funeral procession in London was attended by politicians, nobles and royalty. However, more significantly, thousands of ordinary people joined in, it is estimated seven thousand in Parliament Square alone: mill-workers, flower girls, boot-black boys, costermongers, ragged school children and a host more.

As the cortege passed by, a labouring man with tattered clothes and a piece of torn black crêpe on his arm commented, 'Our Earl's gone! God A'Mighty knows he loved us, and we loved him. We shan't see his likes again.' Perhaps we haven't, but there were many both before and after him who held a passionate Christian care for those in need.

More than one hundred and sixty charitable institutions sent deputations of children and young people to the memorial service in Westminster Abbey on Thursday 8 October 1885; they represented Shaftesbury's widespread and sincere Christian concern for the poor and outcasts. Among them was one organization listed as 'Aged Pilgrims' Friend Society'.

Wednesday September 2nd 1807.

At a meeting of a considerable number of friends to the
intended institution for the relief of the aged and infirm
christian poor in destitute circumstances, held this evening
by adjournment. The following rules &c were agreed upon
First the title Page

The

Aged Pilgrims Friend
Society

Instituted August 12d 1807.

For the Relief of
The Aged and Infirm

Christian Poor

at
Nº 13 Great Bartlee Street
Goswell Street

We know that we have passed from death unto life
because we love the brethren   1 John 3. 14.

Now concerning the collection for the saints as I have
given order to the Churches of Galatia, even so do ye 1 Cor. 16.1

London

Printed by

1807.

The first page in the Society minute book for 12 August 1807

2. The Aged Pilgrims' Friend Society

In 1807 England was midway in its long war with France. It effectively began in 1793 and would continue until Waterloo in 1815 after which Napoleon, the 'Corsican Ogre', was finally exiled to St Helena. The long and costly war was not without its benefits—it was boom time for agriculture. The nation needed bread for its population as well as its army and navy, and the farmers were ready to supply it. However, rising demand was accompanied by rising prices, and no one was hit more severely than the poor for whom bread was the staple food. When the war came to an end, the British government promptly introduced Corn Laws that imposed a heavy duty on the import of all foreign cereals, which simply kept the price of corn high.

'Up north' the industrialists were also making money, because the Napoleonic War coincided with the Industrial Revolution in which Britain led the world by far. Mechanisation brought great wealth to the factory owners, but at the cost of the appalling injuries from unguarded machinery, especially among young children who were cheap labour, and the sprawling and inadequate houses for the workers, which quickly turned into slums.

During the summer of 1807 John Hyatt was preaching through the book of Job. He was co-pastor with Matthew Wilkes and Joel Knight and all three were in charge of the two congregations at 'Whitefield's Tabernacle' in Tottenham Court Road and 'Moorfield's Tabernacle' (also known as 'Whitefield's Tabernacle') in Moorfields at the corner of Tabernacle Street and Leonard Street.

Hyatt was a West Country carpenter from Dorset who, in his teenage years, 'indulged freely in sin until he became a terrible profligate'. He wasted much of his time drinking at the family home of Crosskeys Inn in Sherborne. However, shortly after meeting his future wife Elizabeth

Westcombe he became a Christian—much to his father's disgust—educated himself from the library of his father-in-law and was ordained into the dissenting ministry in 1798. In 1805 Hyatt moved to London and soon became known as a powerful and forthright preacher; his sermons were printed and his preaching tours across the country were eagerly followed. It was said of John Hyatt that 'he feared no man's frown; courted no man's smile; he spoke the whole truth whether men would hear or forbear'.

When John Hyatt arrived in London, immediately he would have felt far removed from the Dorset countryside. His home now was at 61 Great Russell Street and that was close to the city centre. The miserable slums and stinking alleys were only a short walk away. However, maps of this time indicate plenty of green space around the Tabernacle in Moorfields: 'Clover grew round Holloway, the cows of that region grazed amidst golden buttercups, and the skylark was heard in Pentonville.' However, Islington, once known as 'the prettiest village in England', was slowly being engulfed by the sprawling city.

A mission is born

According to the only record of the first meeting of what became the Aged Pilgrims' Friend Society, on **Wednesday evening 5 August 1807** a small group of young men and women met together in the home of Thomas Green at number 8 Peartree Street in Clerkenwell, East London. They had been listening to John Hyatt at Moorfields deliver his midweek lecture from Job 29:12,13 'Because I delivered the poor that cried, and the fatherless, and him that had none to help him. The blessing of him that was ready to perish came upon me: and I caused the widow's heart to sing for joy.'

George Yeoland was present at that meeting; however, he was a military officer about to embark on a long career overseas and therefore his name did not appear among the thirteen founder members a week later. Yeoland retired in 1852 with the rank of Major after twenty-five years of military service, during which he had served under five sovereigns.

On his death on the Isle of Wight at the age of 93, his obituary in *The Mercury* for 16 January 1877 included the fact that on his different stations he acted as Honorary Agent for the British and Foreign Bible Society, the London Missionary Society, the Religious Tract Society, the Naval and Military Society, 'and last, though far from least, he was one of the founders of the Aged Pilgrims' Society.' The obituary added that 'he was a sterling Christian, steadfastly and unflinchingly maintaining, under all circumstances, the honour of his glorious Lord and Master, Jesus Christ.'

Four years before his death he had dictated a description of that first meeting of the Society and this has been the only source of information. With the lapse of more than sixty years, some details of his account may be inaccurate, although there is no good reason to doubt his description of the very first inspiration for the Society.

Yeoland referred to 'the pious zeal of a few young men and maidens, members of the church of Christ connected with the Tabernacle at Moorfields'. After attending the Wednesday evening lecture by the Rev. John Hyatt on the Book of Job in August 1807 they met at the home of Thomas Green, and Yeoland carefully noted that they used the room of the Preparatory School run by Miss Green and 'occupied the forms used by them [the children]'! The army officer commented that they had no 'assistance or intervention' from the three ministers of the Tabernacle 'so its origin and establishment was truly humble and unostentatious'.

Interestingly Yeoland named as present and forming the 'Provisional Committee' one married couple, two single ladies and six men (including himself) plus one whose name he could not recall. There were possibly others present. However, of this Provisional Committee, only Thomas Green—and certainly neither of the two ladies—are named among the twelve founding members at the close of the minutes for Wednesday 12 August 1807. [13]

We do not know what discussions or meetings went on during the next few days. What is certain, however, is that the earliest minute book of the

---

13 George Yeoland's information was contained in a memorandum that he dictated on the Isle of Wight 'in his 90th year of Grace' to Mr M. Murphy, the Secretary of the Society, on 12 November 1873. The document is in the Society archives.

Society records that on **Wednesday evening 12 August 1807** several Christian friends met 'by appointment' at the home of James Bisset, 13 Great Peartree Street, and it was at this meeting that the Society was born. The implication is that there had been a previous informal meeting where a shared concern was expressed; that was the one Yeoland recorded a week earlier.

It is evident from subsequent minutes that the members of this group were already involved in visiting and relieving the sick poor. During these visits they discovered that the 'sick poor' did not include the elderly who were no longer able to work or those who were in long term need, many of whom were left 'wholly desolate'.

At this meeting on 12 August, by common consent James Bisset, the eldest among them at the age of 36 years and a clear minded and at times forceful leader, led a prayer meeting and then spoke movingly of the

James Bisset, co-founder and chairman of the Aged Pilgrims' Friend Society

terrible plight of elderly Christians who often had no family members able or willing to care for them. Nothing is known of Bisset's early life although we do know that in 1818 he preached his first sermon in Stoke Newington from the text: 'The poor have the gospel preached to them.' He subsequently pastored four chapels and on his death in April 1859 at the age of eighty-eight he was buried at Salem Chapel, Hitchin where he had regularly preached.

The minutes of that first meeting acknowledged 'the great number of charitable institutions with which this highly favoured land abounds' but lamented that the aged and infirm Christian poor had been sadly overlooked:

'There are many of this description who, after having spent a laborious life in honest poverty and worn down with old age and bodily infirmity are, in the winter of life, shut up in garrets and cellars, lingering the remainder of their days in distress and wretchedness, deserted by the world among whom they lived as strangers in their better days, and what is still worse they are treated with indifference and neglect by those who are bound by the ties of brotherly love and Christian fellowship to support them. Some of these dear people of God have been found so distressed as to be literally starving with hunger, and no bed to rest their infirm limbs but a little straw on the floor, and without any other covering but what their miserable clothing afforded them.'

After 'prayer to the great head of the church, and mature deliberation', the meeting resolved to form a society: 'exclusively for the purpose of affording permanent relief to the aged and infirm Christian poor of the age of sixty and above and whose income does not exceed five shillings per week'. A pension of five guineas a year would be paid weekly during the remainder of their lives or so long as they continued according to the rules of the society. Subscriptions would be received from 'the public in general and the friends of Christ in particular'. The call was for members of the Christian public to subscribe funds at six pence or more a month to make all this possible.

This plan for a small pension for the elderly infirm preceded by exactly half a century the widely popularised views of John Ruskin[14] and the research and recommendations into poverty by the chocolate manufacturer Joseph Rowntree and his son Seebohm. Among many benefits for his 4,000 employees in York, Rowntree established a Pension Fund in 1906, two years before the Old Age Pension Act was passed by Parliament. The Aged Pilgrims' Friend Society was therefore paying small pensions to the elderly infirm half a century before Ruskin proposed it and one hundred years before the state introduced it.

---

14 In two lectures in Manchester in May 1857, later published as a book entitled *The Political Economy of Art*, the Victorian art and social critic and philosopher, John Ruskin, also proposed the idea of a state old age pension.

The five guineas per annum pension would be in addition to any existing income not exceeding five shillings a week. Five guineas would amount to a little over two shillings a week which meant that it could bring an income up to seven shillings a week. To give perspective for this, a government report for 1843 gave many examples of a family budget among the poorer people, and 42 years old Robert Crick supported himself, his wife and five children on just under 14 shillings (see opposite). His was a precarious existence relying on the meagre contribution of earnings by his wife and three of his children. His own wage of nine shillings a week was entirely spent on bread for the family. Bread, potatoes, tea, sugar, salt, butter and cheese were the only food the Crick family could afford. By comparison, an income for a single elderly Christian of seven shillings a week compared favourably. Besides, unlike Robert Crick, this was a promise for life.

It is to the credit of that small group meeting in East London in August 1807 that their resolve was not only supported by prayer but by the clear teaching of Scripture. They poured out their conviction at that meeting in the following minute:

'The positive command of our Blessed Saviour, the exhortations and practice of the apostles and primitive Christians, the revealed will of God in his word and the nature of our calling unite their voice in saying "Feed the hungry, clothe the naked, do good unto all but especially unto those who are of the household of faith. By this shall all men know that ye are my disciples if ye have love one towards another. He that hath this world's good and seeth his brother (or sister) have need and shutteth up his bowels of compassion from his brother (or sister) how dwelleth the love of God in him?" The Scriptures declare that Christ is the head of the mystical body and that all his people are members one of another. Who is there then that having any one member of his natural body suffer would not do all in his power to relieve it; thus, let us act towards the members of the body mystical; and for our encouragement Jesus has declared that whosoever doth it unto one of the least of these my little ones, does it unto me and that a cup of cold water given unto a disciple in the name of a disciple shall not lose its reward.'

Income and expenditure for the poor in the early 19th century

To appreciate the value of currency in the early 19th century we need to be reminded of the currency used at that time.

There were 12 pennies (d) in one shilling (s), 20 shillings in a pound (£).

Therefore 240 pennies to the pound. A 'guinea' was £1 1s.

The first collection taken up on behalf of the Society was expressed as £20 9s 6d.

But what was the actual value of the currency for the purchase of food and household items?

Depending on the value of the year's harvest, a 4lb loaf of bread (a 'quartern') might cost from 4d to 7d. Bread and potatoes was the staple diet for the poorest families. Bread would take up around half of the family income.

However, below is the report from 1843 providing an example of a weekly budget of the working family of Robert Crick.

It is readily seen here that the father's entire weekly wage paid for bread for the family of seven. A clear example of 'living on the bread line'. For this wage, he probably worked at least ten hours a day for six days.

The Society's pension of five guineas a year or just over two shillings a week can be judged in the light of this. It would certainly provide basic necessities for a single person.

Weekly Income				Weekly Expenditure	
Name	Age	Earnings		Bread	9s 0d
Robert Crick	42	9s 0d		Potatoes	1s 0d
Wife	40	9d		Rent	1s 0d
Boy	12	2s 0d		Tea	2d
Boy	11	1s 0d		Sugar	3½d
Boy	8	1s 0d		Soap	3d
Girl	6	nil		Blue	½d
Boy	4	nil		Thread etc	2d
				Candles	3d
				Salt	½d
				Coal and wood	9d
				Butter	4½d
				Cheese	3d
Total earnings:		**13s 9d**		**Total expenditure:**	**13s 9d**

It was agreed that they would meet again at the same address at 8 o'clock in the evening on Wednesday 2nd September when as many friends as possible would be invited to join and a committee would be chosen; the rules agreed at this current meeting would be submitted to the next meeting. Evidently someone—almost certainly James Bisset—had given a great deal of thought and preparation to this meeting on 12 August 1807.

On **Wednesday 2 September 1807** 'a considerable number of friends' met together and The Aged Pilgrims' Friend Society' was formally born. Thirteen men formed the first committee with James Bisset, whose unswerving commitment to the Society continued for the next fifty years, as secretary, and Thomas Watkins as treasurer. The urgent determination of these pioneers is measured by the fact that from the first meeting to consider the possibility of the work, to the formal appointment of a committee, drawing up the rules of the Society and sending out publicity, little more than a month had elapsed. In March of the following year the first pensioner was entered on the books and two more had been added by the end of the year.

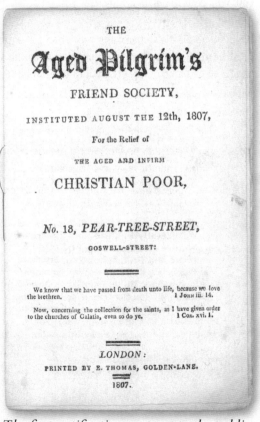

THE

Aged Pilgrim's

FRIEND SOCIETY,

INSTITUTED AUGUST THE 12th, 1807,

For the Relief of

THE AGED AND INFIRM

CHRISTIAN POOR,

No. 18, *PEAR-TREE-STREET,*

GOSWELL-STREET:

We know that we have passed from death unto life, because we love the brethren.   1 JOHN iii. 14.

Now, concerning the collection for the saints, as I have given order to the churches of Galatia, even so do ye.   1 COR. xvi. 1.

LONDON:
PRINTED BY E. THOMAS, GOLDEN-LANE.
1807.

The first notification sent out to the public for the formation of the Aged Pilgrims' Friend Society. The apostrophe in 'Pilgrim's' on this notice was, presumably, a misprint

It was unanimously agreed by the meeting to circulate to the public the appeal contained in the minutes of the previous meeting and the rules of the Society. Subsequently an article outlining the purpose for the Society was sent to the *Evangelical Magazine*, who printed it in their supplement for the year 1807; an extract was published in the weekly religious newspaper the *Instructor*.

Eighteen rules were drawn up by The Aged Pilgrims' Friend Society. Here is a summary:

- The support was for those who showed good evidence of a true Christian faith, were aged sixty and above (that age almost certainly influenced by Leviticus 27:7) and whose present income was not more than five shillings a week (though stated in 1838 as six shillings a week exclusive of rent).[15] They would be given five guineas a year, paid weekly at two shillings. This would be paid for life, providing they remained in the faith, their other income had not increased and they were not found to be living 'in any known sin'.

- Subscriptions were invited for a minimum of six pence a month, and subscribers could nominate people deserving support from the society.

- A committee not exceeding thirteen and not less than five would be elected annually.

- All those receiving support would be visited each month by a member of the committee, who themselves must be wholly committed Christians since: 'no person may be appointed to visit the Lord's family but such as are of the household of faith and whose known principles are strictly consistent with the word of God.'

- A General Meeting would be held twice a year to which all subscribers were invited, 'a minister requested to give an exhortation, and a collection made'.

---

15 The thirty-first annual report of the committee (1838), p. 6.

- Various housekeeping issues were included concluding with the fact that: 'all meetings of the committee and the society begin and end with prayer.' This was amended in 1919 to 'All meetings shall begin by reading a portion of Scripture and prayer, and end with prayer.'

See Appendix A for the full text of the eighteen Rules for the Society.

With the reasonable expectation that the number of applicants would greatly exceed the income of the Society, a careful method of selection was adopted. All subscribers could nominate someone whom they considered in need of help; details would be given to the committee who would then send two or three members to interview the candidate. At each committee meeting the number of new pensioners they could admit, according to the income of the Society, would be decided from the Accepted Candidates. From the names before them, the appropriate number would be chosen by casting a lot. Interestingly, Andrew Reed's method of electing children eligible for his London orphanage six years later was almost identical to that established by the Aged Pilgrims' Friend Society.

In December 1827 it was agreed that all subscribers should be allowed a number of votes in proportion to the size of their subscription and that the subscribers would vote on the Accepted Candidates to be offered a pension. This super democracy is illustrated in June 1828 when 1000 copies listing all candidates for election, plus a ballot paper, plus a book of rules, would be sent 'to every subscriber listed to vote'.

Growing pains

In general, church leaders were at first hesitant to support this infant Society. The first two ministers invited declined; one would only add his name if other ministers had already done so. It was left to the faithful John Hyatt, whose sermon at Moorfields Tabernacle had inspired the founding of the Society, to write an address in October 1808; 750 copies were printed. John Hyatt was more than willing also to preach at the general meeting in December, though for some unspecified reason the managers of the Tabernacle felt unable to grant the use of the building for that purpose.

In January 1809 members of the committee reported that they had managed to persuade the Minister of Hope Street in Spitalfields to make his chapel available, but only after the assurance that John Hyatt would be preaching! When John Hyatt felt obliged to pull out of his commitment, due to the pressure of his busy preaching programme, Hope Street Chapel was withdrawn. The committee then approached Mr Branch of Bunhill Row Chapel who was more than willing for the Society to use the chapel, though this was never used.

From February to September the committee members approached six churches or meeting places and, for a variety of reasons, none was available. Finally, in September when St Anne's, Blackfriars refused 'without assigning any reason', the committee decided not to make any further applications 'until a convenient opportunity offers'. By June 1810, that opportunity arose when John Hyatt expressed the fact that although his diary was fully engaged for the next six months, after that he was more than willing to preach for the Society. The challenge of finding both ministers and the managers of a building agreeable to allow the Society the use of their premises continued for many years. In April 1825 the committee reported that although the churchwardens of Christ Church, Newgate were willing to make the church building available for the Society's anniversary, the vicar withdrew the offer.

It was always the policy of the Society to relieve members of the household of faith irrespective of their denominational affiliation. They did not want to be seen purely as a society for the care of nonconformist Christians. However, the fact that the charity began with, and was largely run by, nonconformists did not recommend it to many in the Established church. In 1827 committee members were urged to do all they could to encourage ministers of the Established church to give assistance at the annual meeting.

One encouragement, however, was the editor of the *Instructor* who regularly advertised the mission in his weekly religious newspaper.

Apparently, the committee members were finding it difficult to visit each pensioner personally to give them their two shillings a week; in March 1809 it was therefore resolved that the pensioners themselves would have to collect their pension on the first Thursday of every month from the Committee Room, presumably at the home of James Bisset at 13 Great Peartree Street. If they were prevented by illness or infirmity, only then would a committee member visit personally. A year later it was noted that several pensioners were so weak and infirm that they were unable to collect their pension and the committee was forced to return to the original arrangement of visitors personally delivering the pension.

A Visitor bringing the pension to an elderly Pilgrim. ('Inasmuch' 1807-1907)

Collecting the subscriptions, which might be offered weekly or monthly, was another time-consuming aspect of the work. To overcome this a Collector was appointed and was allowed 5% of subscriptions collected. However, this caused its own problems and in June 1828 Mr Adams presented 'a long and acrimonious letter' of complaint to the committee. He was invited to attend the committee, though apparently he never did so, and the issue rumbled on for nineteen months until he was finally replaced, though not until he had been so insolent to two subscribers that they had withdrawn their support.

Another problem confronting the infant Society was that their system of subscribers voting for those who were Accepted Candidates for the pension meant that occasionally there was evidence of canvassing for votes and, as proxy voting was allowed, this was open to abuse. With the best of intentions, subscribers were anxious that their nominations should be awarded a pension. It was certainly not an ideal process, and as late as 1878 John Gadsby, the son of William Gadsby the hymn writer and leader among the Strict Baptists, openly advertised in *The Gospel Standard* that if Subscribers would entrust him with their proxy votes he would be able to ensure the election of certain elderly Christians.

Inevitably, there were occasional grumblings and complaints from subscribers concerning various practical aspects of the ministry, but to the credit of the committee they were always ready to invite such complainants to their meeting in order to explain their problem and allow the committee to discuss it. On one occasion the minute let slip the fact that a complainant was 'heard with great patience'!

Pastoral care

From the very beginning, the Society commenced and concluded all their meetings in prayer, and their concern for the honour of God in every aspect of their work is clear. It was never intended that the Aged Pilgrims' Friend Society would be a charity merely to gather and dispense money for elderly Christians in need. A minute of the committee in December 1832 stressed the importance of every pensioner receiving a pastoral visit each month, and that the visitor would ensure that, especially to those who might be discouraged, spiritual care was given through helpful conversation, the reading of the Scriptures and prayer. Much later in the century Dr Doudney, Vicar of St Luke's, Bedminster, produced a tiny booklet (6 cm × 9 cm) to encourage the residents of Pilgrim Homes. Under the title: *Words for the Weary and Worn; to the inmates of the Aged Pilgrims' Friend Society's Asylums* it was priced at 'one Half-Penny'.

Since all committee members were expected to visit the pensioners and pray with them, a problem presented itself when in December 1832 Mr Seaman expressed himself willing to serve the Society in any way he could. He was an able man, clearly a spiritual Christian, and a regular attender at church. His one problem was that he had never been able to pray publicly, not even with his own family. The committee members who visited him 'urged upon him to try, and thought that by attempting he might surmount the difficulty under which he seemed to labour'. Mr Seaman felt that since this was a rule of the Society and he was unable to commit to this, he withdrew his availability for the committee. In this case, the committee was so certain of his value to them that they nevertheless unanimously accepted him as a member.

It is a neat reflection on the thoughtfulness of the committee that at their meeting on 27 December 1825 they expressed warm appreciation to Mr and Mrs Carman for the hospitality of their home for committee meetings, and they resolved to give ten shillings to the house servants 'for the trouble the committee have given them'. This was repeated over the next two years, but thereafter, presumably to avoid the money being taken from Society funds, a donation was made by committee members themselves. Perhaps the servants well-earned that little extra income because in addition, a monthly prayer meeting was established for the last Friday of each month at 'seven o'clock precisely'. This prayer meeting was specifically 'to implore the blessing of the Lord on the society' and would also be held at the home of the Carmans. Another prayer meeting, every other Friday, would be held in various homes. They were convinced that the work of the Society must be covered continually by the prayers of those responsible for its running and by its supporters.

All candidates for a pension came in person to the annual meeting where votes were cast. This meant that some inevitably went away disappointed having spent the best part of a day waiting for the outcome. A committee minute for 1828 reveals that the committee themselves took up a subscription for the twenty-five unsuccessful candidates and gave them two shillings and three pence each in compensation.

At each meeting the committee reviewed those who had been visited as candidates for the pension fund. Sometimes their testimony was recorded in detail, but mostly it was brief and concluded with the fact that they were either approved or not. What mattered most to the committee was that each pensioner should have a sincere and genuine experience of Jesus

Christ as their Lord and Saviour; simply 'a good moral character' was not enough. It helped if they had a clear understanding of the Christian faith, but this was not essential; it was saving faith that mattered. Ann Hann, who received three shillings a week from the parish supplemented by 8d from her own needlework, was recommended despite having 'many confused ideas'.

Not only confused ideas but a less than robust confidence in God would not necessarily debar a needy person from a pension. Oakley Briggs, aged 72, earned four shillings a week labouring (all of which went on his rent) and an extra two shillings as a pew opener in his chapel, 'his wife being confined to her bed and one daughter insane'. The visitors' report added that Oakley had known the Lord for many years and had come under a deep conviction of sin even though he still had many fears. At the close of the visit 'he engaged in prayer with much simplicity, but with very feeble sense of the Lord's forgiveness of his sin or enjoyment of the love of God in his soul.'

The committee, unashamedly Reformed in their theology, occasionally betrayed their disdain for Arminian views when commenting that William Higgins, although a member at a Wesleyan Connection Chapel, was not intolerant of other views of the gospel. He was accepted.

In March 1809 two pensioners were added and it is evident that not all were drawn from the immediate locality of the committee, since the list of potential candidates included Henry Pennicud whose only address was 'opposite the church. Lewisham'—that was on the south side of the Thames. The number of applicants was slowly growing. However, the visitors discovered that two of the seven hopefuls at this meeting in March were found to be 'totally ignorant of a divine change and of themselves as sinners, and of Jesus Christ as a Saviour'. A year later, two pensioners were discovered having an adequate income from elsewhere that had not been disclosed to the committee and their pension was withdrawn.

Although the original rules stated that if a pensioner went into the Workhouse, their pension would cease since they would be provided for in the Workhouse, the committee apparently took pity on Mary Dobson, and even though she had gone into the Workhouse they continued to pay her a shilling a week for tea and sugar.

The early minute books of the Aged Pilgrims' Friend Society presented short cameos of some of the pensioners adopted by the Society.

Martha Summerhill lived in Peter Street, Soho on four shillings a week, half of which went on her rent.

John Richards and his wife had lost £4,000 invested in a woollen factory in the West of England and now existed on just three shillings a week.

Sarah Davis was the widow of a lieutenant in the Navy whose naval pension ceased on his death. Now aged 74 and having lost the use of one hand, she could no longer do the needlework that provided her a little income; Sarah lodged with her niece and was entirely dependent on a few friends to help her.

Sarah Knight at the age of 76 had been blind for 12 years. Long Acre Chapel was her spiritual home 'but being blind I cannot go there as I used to do, having no person to lead me and none to read the Scriptures to me. This obliges me to sit most of my time alone, which frequently makes me dull and low.'

Quogo Cavillore, was a 77-year-old African. He and his wife existed on an income of just two shillings a week and his rent paid by a few friends. He had been convicted of his sin in New York when, at the age of 22, he attended a place of worship with some companions intending to disturb the meeting. Something the preacher from England said so convicted him that he trusted Christ and his life was transformed.

These are typical of the pensioners in the early days of the mission, and they sadly reveal how little the churches provided for those who, through age and infirmity, were unable to attend a place of worship. All of them were adherents to a Christian church, but none of them was cared for in any adequate way. Thankfully, this was not the case of every church or minister in London.

By Midsummer 1810 the Society held a balance of just over £55 and made the interesting decision to invest this in government stock!

A group of Lady Visitors in 1907

3. The Ladies' Auxiliary

In 1821 a committee of Lady Visitors was formed to visit the female pensioners, promote the work of the Society—particularly in encouraging subscriptions—and later to visit the residents of the various Pilgrim Homes.

The role of women throughout the Victorian era is well documented. For centuries women in the labouring agricultural community worked the land alongside their men, as well as caring for the children, keeping the home, and often engaging in some form of cottage industry to help supplement the meagre income of the men and boys. It was a hard life of drudgery from first light to the end of the day, but no less so for the men. With the advent of the Industrial Revolution towards the end of the 18th century, the tide of humanity that moved from the countryside to the rapidly expanding cities changed all that. Now, the men had to 'commute' to their place of work and their wives remained at home to care for the ever-growing brood of children.

Among the middle-class tradesmen, life was much the same, although the lot of the woman was more comfortable. If her husband was moderately prosperous she could afford one or more servants to do the housework, cook meals, and even care for the children. This allowed the wife more time to herself, providing she carefully followed the instructions of Mrs Beeton to check regularly the accounts and ensure that the servants did everything in the proper manner.[16]

For the women in the homes of the wealthy gentry, life was very different. They had little to do but to prepare for their anticipated, and mostly arranged, marriage by learning how to be an attractive catch and

---

16 In 1861 Isabella Beeton's husband, Samuel, published *Mrs Beeton's Book of Household Management*, although it had appeared since 1859 in monthly instalments. After her death in 1865 it continued to be published as *Mrs Beeton's Cookery Book* and was added to until the original 43 chapters became 74 in 2,000 pages. It was hugely popular until well after the Great War.

subsequently a dutiful wife. Her ability in music, art, French and perhaps a smattering of polite religion, would certainly help her, but above all she must be feminine and submissive and manage the servants well.

It would have been almost exclusively from the second of these groups that the Lady Visitors were drawn. With a little more time to spare, the wives of relatively prosperous tradesmen, merchants or bankers were eager to find useful outlets for their undoubted gifts. In fact, they became a dangerous class in the eyes of many politicians. Some of them were well educated and erudite, even writing novels and political statements, and above all demanding women's right to vote.

The Quakers had long held their women in equality, and John Wesley allowed women to be preachers and leaders of local Methodist classes: 'God owns women in the conversion of sinners, and who am I that I should withstand God?', and the independent churches generally allowed women a full voice and vote in their congregational meetings.

However, whatever her status in life, the woman's role throughout the Victorian era was subordinate and inferior to the men. Even in the middle of the century Charlotte Brontë expressed the frustration of many women through her heroine Jane Eyre:

'Women are supposed to be very calm generally. But women feel just as men feel; they need exercise for their faculties and a field for their efforts as much as their brothers do; they suffer from too rigid a restraint, too absolute a stagnation, precisely as men would suffer; and it is narrow-minded in their more privileged fellow-creatures to say that they ought to confine themselves to making puddings and knitting stockings, to playing on the piano and embroidering bags.'

The law was heavily stacked against her freedom. However cruelly treated, divorce was virtually impossible for her; few working class women would have any formal education, everything she owned belonged to her husband on marriage, she could not open a bank account or contract any form of business without her husband's consent. Only in 1878 was the first woman allowed to study in the University of London. It would be well into the next century (1928) before women were allowed to vote in national elections.

A Ladies' Committee

Against this background we can understand the relationship between the main Committee of the Society and the Ladies' Committee. Minutes of its precise formation have been lost, although we do know that a Ladies' Committee was established in 1821; from thereon they made a valuable contribution to the work of the Society. The names of the ladies are regularly listed in the minutes of the monthly meetings of the Society and their visits to the Life Pensioners, Approved Candidates, and even those in the workhouse, illustrated the Society's pastoral care of those in their charge.

Every pensioner and Approved Candidate was visited by a committee member each month in addition to the visits of the ladies. The minutes of 31 December 1832 laid emphasis upon the fact that all visitors should consider it 'a special part of their duty in visiting the poor of the household of faith to administer spiritual consolation to their often dejected and cast down spirits by conversation and reading the Scriptures and engaging in prayer'. Among the many situations detailed in the early records, it is sad to read of an elderly blind saint 'in her daily solitude and depression, with no friends or relatives to make life easier or brighter for her'. It was undoubtedly the regular, often twice a month, visits by the ladies that brought light into the otherwise harsh world of so many like this.

By now there were at least twenty men on the main Committee and between forty and fifty ladies on theirs.

The earliest surviving reference to the Ladies' Committee is in March 1826 when it was reported that a few members of the Ladies' Committee had withdrawn from the Society and that for 'several months' they had been secretly forming an alternative society with similar purposes. Within a month it was noted that ten more ladies had joined the new society although that still left twenty-eight members of the Ladies' Committee. This newly formed society, known as the Aged Female Christians Friend Society, appears to have closed some twenty years later.

No reason for this dissension is given, although it is very likely that they objected to the fact that, many churches being closed to them, some public meetings of the Society were held in local taverns. The previous year the Society's meeting had been held in the Crown and Anchor in the Strand and the eight resolutions, with two speakers to each, must have ensured that the meeting continued late into the evening. In January 1826 it had been reported to the committee that at the last meeting of the Ladies' Committee a resolution had been passed 'that some of the Ladies are of the opinion that the interests of the Society will be promoted by discontinuing the Annual Meetings as heretofore'—presumably a reference to meetings in taverns.

Although the word Teetotal probably originated with the Preston Temperance Society in 1833, already a call to total abstention from alcohol because of its tragic effects upon the poor, was gaining ground across England. Perhaps significantly it was at the same meeting in March 1826 that the Committee cancelled its booking at the City of London Tavern and agreed in future only to hold its meetings in places of public worship.

It is to the credit of the main Committee that they minuted to take 'no other notice' of this secret planning among a few of the Ladies' Committee other than to acknowledge the 'impropriety of such conduct'.

The ladies were certainly expressing the new-found self-confidence of women in the early 19th century. Their resolution, and the reasons behind it, had persuaded the main Committee to change course on the venue of its meetings. However, it also presented a potential conflict between the two committees, and two years later, in February 1828, a meeting was held to clarify the relationship between the Ladies' Committee and the main Committee of the Society. Clearly some confusion had arisen when the Ladies and the main Committee disagreed.

Foreseeing that this could present significant problems in the future, since two committees could not run one organisation, it was suggested the ladies form themselves into an Auxiliary Committee. As such they would have no executive say in the proceedings of the main Committee. Significantly, however, the main Committee offered that if the ladies wished to take a more prominent involvement in the decisions of the Society, they would be welcome to become members of the main Committee and attend all the meetings because 'it is highly inconsistent and contrary to all practice to have two acting committees of one society'.

Auxiliaries

In response, the ladies decided to designate themselves: 'The Ladies' Auxiliary Committee of the Aged Pilgrims' Friend Society'. However, they did suggest that whilst relinquishing any right to interfere in the management of the Society they must retain the right to make their views known on important issues and that their views would be inserted into the minute book of the main Committee. Rule five of the Ladies' Auxiliary made it clear that any alteration in the existing rules of the Society must have the agreement of both committees before it could be implemented.

The Committee expressed to the ladies the 'great pleasure they have experienced in the mutual and amicable termination of their consultations, and especially in the very excellent and truly Christian spirit by which the ladies have been activated in coming to such a desirable decision'. This may sound patronising to modern ears, but it must be understood in the light of the early 19th century when, in the greater part of society, the woman's voice was neither heard nor wanted. In April 1827 when the ladies complained of a supporters' meeting of which they had not been informed, they received a full and abject apology from the men.

Regional Auxiliaries were formed to supplement the work of the Ladies' Auxiliary Committee. The first of these Auxiliaries was formed at Grove Chapel in Camberwell in the 1830s under the encouragement of the Minister Joseph Irons. By the turn of the century there were twenty-one Auxiliaries across the nation though mainly concentrated in the south. They were almost exclusively the province of ladies and they did a valuable work on behalf of the Society in visiting the pensioners, providing outings and treats for them, and later acting as collectors for the subscriptions. Subsequently, they would make a significant contribution both in the support of the residents and in the running of the Pilgrim Homes.

It was the Auxiliaries that commenced the popular sales of work. At first there was some concern from the main Committee that they may be too much like the bazaars of the world, but the scruples were overcome with the suggestion that they should be simply for 'the sale of home-made goods and fancy work'. Throughout the 20th century they were particularly popular and were invariably mentioned in the *Quarterly Record* of the Society. Always concerned for the reputation of the Aged Pilgrims' Friend Society, in 1923 rules were implemented to govern the sales of work. These prohibited fancy dress costumes, mock auctions and anything that would seem to mimic worldly bazaars. In addition, no items were to be sold in which only a percentage was donated to the Society.

Grove Chapel Camberwell, London. Built in 1819 for the congregation of Joseph Irons, it was here that the first Auxiliary was formed in 1835

The Annual Report of 1838 commended the Ladies' Auxiliary Committee for their 'Long continued, zealous, and cordial assistance in visiting a large number of the female pensioners and in obtaining a considerable number of Subscribers and Donors, for which the society is highly indebted.' Years later when Lord Shaftesbury was presiding over an annual meeting of the Society he unashamedly commented, 'This is pre-eminently the age of the ministry of women.'

Seven decades later nothing had changed. The report of 1910 specifically expressed appreciation for the 'invaluable services of the Lady Visitors' across the country. Their work included distributing the pensions, attending to sales of work, administering the Benevolent Funds of the Homes, and regularly visiting the residents. However, one of their more arduous duties was to collect the subscriptions. At this time, long before Direct Debits, Standing Orders or the wide use of postal cheques, Collectors had to be employed to gather the subscriptions promised. It was noted that sometimes they received 'a cool reception', and it certainly involved a large amount of simple foot slogging. One lady in Sussex commented that she could walk up to twenty miles in one day to make collections, and after nineteen days collecting, she needed a rest! She had 'used up my strength for the present; just enough and none to spare; truly God is good'.

Significantly they are described as 'honorary' Collectors. This change ensured that the acrimonious relationship with Mr Adams who was paid 5% of his collections back in 1828 would never be repeated! The position of paid Collectors was ended in 1892.

Part of the first home of the Aged Pilgrims' Friend Society at Camberwell

4. Homes for the elderly

Perhaps the earliest reference to an almshouse is found from an unexpected source. A Greek inscription on a wall of the Old City of Jerusalem next to the Bab es Sahera Gate (Herod's Gate) mentions John and Berine (Verina) from Constantinople who established a *gerokomion* (an old age home) for the poor elderly.[17] This was dedicated to the Virgin Mary and is dated around AD 400. Even before this, it is known that Helena (AD 250-330), the Christian mother of the Emperor Constantine, opened the first Roman 'nursing home' for the elderly. Helena 'encouraged nurses to become especially skilled in what we now call gerontological nursing'.[18]

However, in the modern period, the idea of almshouses for the elderly poor reaches back to the 10th century. During the mediaeval period homes, or hospitals, for the elderly poor were frequently linked with chantries where masses were paid to be sung (chanted) on behalf of the dead, or paid for by gifts from the rich to earn merit in the afterlife. The first recorded almshouse is found in York in the 10th century at the time of King Athelstan, but the oldest building still standing is dated around the year 990 in Worcester.

By the mid-16th century there were 800 'hospitals' but many were chantries tied to monasteries and these were lost in the dissolution of the monasteries after Henry's Act of Supremacy in 1534. Almshouses dating back at least 400 years can still be found scattered liberally across the country. In 1563 justices of the peace were empowered to raise compulsory funds on the parish for the relief of the poor; this was reaffirmed in 1597 and stayed in place until the Poor Law Amendment Act of 1834.

---

17 First discovered in 1863 but later transcribed and translated by Charles Clermont-Garneau, *Archaeological researches in Palestine during the years 1873-1873*, pp. 246-248. The gate is also known in the Hebrew as the 'Flower Gate'.
18 Quoted in *Servant Leadership in Nursing* by Mary Elizabeth O'Brien (Sudbury, Massachusetts: Jones and Bartlett Publishers, 2011), p. 36.

London Almshouses

*Sackville College is a Jacobean Almshouse founded by Robert
Sackville in 1609 and still in use as an almshouse today.
July 26, 2015, East Grinstead, Sussex*

In 1633 the Fishmongers' Almshouses were built opposite the Elephant and Castle in London but were demolished in 1859 for the construction of Spurgeon's Metropolitan Tabernacle. Spurgeon opened almshouses for seventeen elderly women, but that was not until well beyond the middle of the century. In 1714 the Ironmongers' Company built homes for fifty pensioners at Shoreditch. These are now the Geffrye Museum of the Home. In 1730 Charles Hopton left money in his will to build twenty-six almshouses for 'poor decayed men'.

Many who endowed almshouses would otherwise be unknown to future generations. A memorial in Bath Abbey erected by his widow, informs us that Fletcher Partis, who died in August 1820—just five years before the Aged Pilgrims' Friend Society first discussed in committee their plan for a home for the elderly—not only supported several public charities during his life but also provided 'an Asylum for thirty decayed Gentlewomen being Widows or Daughters of Clergymen, Merchants, or Professional Men, whom adverse fortune had deprived of brighter prospects, where he hoped they would find rest and comfort in the evening of their days'. That Fletcher Partis was a true Christian is evidenced by his hope that 'through the sufferings of his blessed Saviour he should obtain that mercy which is promised to all truly repentant sinners'.

Over the centuries, thousands of almshouses were built around the country. Until 1834 relief of poverty was left to individual parishes, which might work fairly well in many rural areas, but in overcrowded London poverty was simply overwhelming and the number of homes for the elderly who could no longer work was woefully inadequate. During the 19th century homes for around 650 elderly residents were built by various charities in London and this, together with existing almshouses, meant that by the end of the century almost two thousand elderly were being cared for.[19] But thousands more were still left out in the cold.

Behind the Poor Law Amendment Act of 1834 was the thought that previous poor laws, which had lasted for 200 years, encouraged the idle.

---

19 These figures are taken from the index of almshouses in London in *The London Almshouses— six centuries of housing for the aged* (published by The Housing Centre, London c. 1944).

These laws would be swept away by making work obligatory on the poor in order to discourage 'loafers'. Sadly, this only increased the fear of the infamous Workhouse where husbands and wives, parents and children were separated, where the healthy in mind lived alongside the severely insane, where work was hard, tedious and soul destroying, food was generally little above the starvation level, heating even in winter was minimal and the inmates had little hope of release. To be pitied above them all were the elderly and infirm.

London Workhouses in the 19th century

In the event, the Act did little more than make a bad situation worse. It was implemented firmly in the south of the country, but in the North there was strong opposition, including riots, and it fed the growing influence of Chartism. In 1839, Thomas Carlyle wrote: 'The new Poor Law is an announcement ... that whosoever will not work ought not to live. Can the poor man that is willing to work always find work and live by his work? A man willing but unable to find work is ... the saddest thing under the sun.' Worse than this were the elderly infirm who were quite unable to work. The workhouse system continued until 1930.

A home for Pilgrims

Although the pensions of the Aged Pilgrims' Friend Society were undoubtedly a lifeline for many destitute elderly Christians, it still frequently left them with wholly inadequate shelter and the ever-present spectre of the Workhouse for their final days. The driving force of the Society is worth repeating:

'After having spent a laborious life in poverty, and worn out with old age and bodily infirmity are, in the winter of life, shut up in garrets and cellars lingering the remainder of their days in distress and wretchedness, deserted by the world ... And neglected by those of the same household of faith of which they are members ... Some of these dear aged Pilgrims have been found so distressed as to be almost starving with hunger, and destitute of clothing or any bed to rest their infirm limbs except a little straw on the floor, and without any covering but what few rags they had on afforded them.'[20]

Some members of the Society had been considering the subject for several years, and a special meeting was held on Tuesday 13 December 1825 when the twelve members considered, 'The propriety of erecting almshouses for a certain number of pensioners on the society.' The immediate concern was that such a project might seriously affect the general funds to provide pensions; by this year the Society had supported more than 800 pensioners and raised over £15,000. The committee met again on 20 December for

---

20 From the foundation document of the Aged Pilgrims' Friend Society, 1807.

'further consideration of building an asylum for connected Pilgrims who are Pensioners in the Society'. It was agreed to build 'Twenty small houses each to contain four convenient separate apartments.' It would be known as The Aged Pilgrims' Asylum.

To modern ears the word 'asylum' is unfortunate and it was probably an unfortunate use of the term even in 1825. Little was understood of the causes of mental illness, and anyone suffering from a range of symptoms from depression, imbecility or senile dementia could be sent into an 'asylum'. Perhaps the most notorious at this time was in Wakefield, Yorkshire, where the treatment of patients was cruelly inhumane. But here in London things were only marginally better. The infamous Bethlehem Hospital—shortened to 'Bedlam' which became a description of uproar and confusion—had been relocated to Southwark in 1815, but it would be some time before its reputation was erased as a place where 'lunatics' were incarcerated and forgotten by their families and where members of the public could pay to come and watch—and even bait—the antics of the inmates at teatime on Sunday.[21]

However, the word 'asylum' originally meant nothing more than an institution to care for those in need, and that is what the Society intended. This 'suitable asylum or alms houses' would be free from rent and where the aged Pilgrims could 'end the toils and cares of their earthly pilgrimage in comparative ease and tranquillity'.

A separate fund would be set up to buy a freehold site within three miles of St Paul's Cathedral. Trustees would be chosen by the subscribers; once again, this democracy reflected the dissenting and congregational churchmanship of most of those on the committee. Copies of an advertisement would be printed, and advertisements would be placed in the *Evangelical Magazine* and the *Christian Observer*. A graphic description of the conditions endured by many aged pilgrims was contained in the advertisement:

---

21 The original Bethlehem Hospital was attached to the priory of St Mary of Bethlehem in Bishopsgate, London and received its first 'lunatics' in 1377. The hospital was transferred to Moorfields in 1675 and was infamous as a place where visitors could 'enjoy' the antics of the lunatics. This continued into the 18th century until it was moved to Southwark.

'One of the bitterest ingredients in the cup of sorrow and poverty to aged pious Christians, is the miserable habitations to which their necessitous circumstances compel them to resort for a temporary dwelling place. A dark damp kitchen underground or an obscure garret at the top of an old house in an unhealthy situation commonly hides from the view of the world and from the notice of their fellow travellers to the heavenly country, one who has seen brighter days, and who has in former years been a housekeeper in comfortable or affluent circumstances. Others have spent their past life in honest and respectable servitude, while they had strength to labour and who were then strangers to the painful privations and wretched abodes which the death of their former helpmates, or the infirmities of old age, have reduced them, and where they are compelled to seek a precarious and insufficient shelter for their trembling limbs and sinking frame, in the dreary winter of declining life.'

That would be a significant pull on the heartstrings of Christians in Victorian England.

Ten rules were set out for the proper governing of the asylum: these included setting up a separate committee (though responsible to the parent Committee) to govern its affairs, and the wise use of the finances and the property itself. Nine rules set out how the residents would be chosen and five related to the Warden. There were also 'Rules for the Inmates': they must keep their rooms tidy, not undertake any cottage industry nor bang nails or pegs into the walls; health permitting they must attend at a place of worship and they must refrain from any unnecessary work on the Lord's day; fires and candles must be extinguished by ten pm at which hour (one hour earlier in the winter) the main gate would be locked.

In this year (1825) the original rules of the parent Committee were revised and increased from eighteen to thirty-two, and it was felt advisable to draw up a basis of faith on which both the Society and Asylum were conducted. This was finally adopted in 1833.

The TRUTHS OF REVELATION,
Agreeable to which the affairs of this Society and its Asylum are conducted,
are these:

That the Scriptures of the Old and New Testament are the only rule of faith and practice: the unity of God, in three co-equal and co-eternal persons, the Father, the Word, and the Holy Ghost; the essential divinity and sinless humanity of Jesus Christ; as God-man Mediator; the Godhead and personality of the Holy Ghost; the fall of man by sin; the efficacious grace of God; redemption by Jesus Christ, and justification by his blood and righteousness; regeneration and sanctification by the Holy Spirit; the final perseverance of the saints; the general resurrection and judgement of all men; the eternal bliss of saints; and the everlasting punishment of the wicked.

A room in the Camberwell home

The Camberwell home

The first public meeting in support of this new project was held at Spa Fields Chapel, Clerkenwell on 23 October 1826 and raised £435. However, not until April 1833 was a suitable site donated to the Society in Southampton Street, Camberwell, two and a half miles across the river from St Paul's Cathedral and then a quiet, semi-rural location.

The original plan had been for a home for eighty pensioners. This was reduced to sixty and finally to forty-two. Building commenced in October 1834 and single rooms for twenty residents were complete by the following June. At the dedication of these new homes, a marble tablet was placed on the site with the simple inscription 'A.P.A., 16th Oct.,1834, 1 Samuel vii.12'. A shortage of money delayed completion of the home, and work did not recommence until 1837—the year in which the eighteen-year-old Princess Victoria took the throne of the British Empire on the death of her uncle William IV.

Camberwell provided a secure and peaceful home for hundreds of pilgrims for 120 years, though not without its problems. In the early days, the asylum committee had to contend with blocked drains, an unhealthy water supply, and blowback from smoky chimneys; there was even the challenge of local youths throwing stones at the building—the police were informed and a reward of 10 shillings was offered to anyone who could report the culprits. In September 1836 the Visiting Committee reported on the fact that some 'inmates' were dressed rather unbecomingly for their age and status and they were given a short lecture on scripture references for appropriate dress. Later, when a few residents decorated their rooms with wallpaper, they were told to remove it forthwith!

In addition to the general management and oversight of the home and the well-being of its residents, the rules relating to the Warden included the instruction that he or she should 'manifest all Christian attention and kindness towards its inhabitants' each of whom should be visited at least once a week. They were also encouraged to watch out for any visitors who might be 'suspicious or disreputable characters'.[22] Nothing has changed there!

Those who were considered in need of such a home were listed, and when a vacancy occurred a system similar to the voting for pensions was followed. Some years later the Ladies' Committee suggested that a fairer and more pastorally sensitive system would be to take those who had been on the list longest to fill a vacancy. The ladies clearly had wisdom on their side but unfortunately the suggestion was not adopted. From the perspective of today, perhaps the wisest solution would have been to give priority to those who had the greatest need. In 1866 during an election for fifteen residents at Camberwell there was evidence of subscribers soliciting votes on behalf of their preferred candidate.

Even before the home was opened, the Ladies' Committee recognised that many residents would need regular visiting and care; to this end, in November 1835 they formed a Female Visiting Committee. They met every Thursday to discuss the needs of the residents, and as winter approached, blankets, flannel, flannel petticoats and stockings were supplied; some of the ladies knitted woollen socks for the residents. The watchful attention of the visiting ladies, and the care of the residents for one another, meant that the reports show many acts of kindness to those who were infirm or seriously ill. Occasionally outings were arranged for the residents.

However, all was not always as sweet and light as later histories preferred to suggest. This haven of peace was occasionally shattered by squabbles and grumbling among the residents, even some cases of minor pilfering, and over the years a few had to be removed from the home for drunkenness! In the Spring of 1827, the unruly behaviour, profane language and abuse of her husband by one of the pensioners, Mrs Deane, came to the attention of the committee. She was asked to attend the next meeting to explain herself. She did not attend and, as many neighbours were complaining, her pension was withdrawn. Mrs Deane persuaded someone to write on her behalf, protesting that an enemy was causing trouble for her, but the complaints were too many and varied.

---

22 The published record of 1838, p. 58.

We may suspect that poor Mrs Deane was suffering from dementia, but it was not understood back then. A meeting of the committee as early as 25 February 1810 provides perhaps the first hint of dementia among the pensioners: 'Mrs Millway had been deranged in her head and was removed in the course of this month to the workhouse.' It would be another seventy years before the Bavarian doctor Aloysius Alzheimer identified what we understand today as dementia.

However, these uncommon incidents must be seen in the light of the hundreds who lived peacefully in the home over the course of 150 years.

In 1854 a Benevolent Fund was opened to provide extra help for the residents in times of sickness 'and other seasons of emergency'. Some were already bedridden and requiring medical assistance and nursing care. The commencement of a Coal Fund ensured a regular supply of coal for each of the residents.

The Society had always been careful to maintain its completely nondenominational stance. Irrespective of their church affiliation, the elderly poor were equally considered for pensions and for residence in the homes. Although generally the largest group at any one time came from Baptist churches, other Independents and members of the Church of England were well represented.[23]

However, like its residents, the building grew old and a report in 1957 admitted that it would be judged 'old fashioned'.[24] With ever-increasing health and safety regulations and the high cost of maintaining an aging building, the home struggled on until 1990 when it had to be closed.

The Hornsey Rise home

In the Golden Jubilee year of the founding of the Society an even larger home was proposed. By now over 400 pensioners were supported. An appeal was launched but it took another eleven years before two acres of land could be purchased at Hornsey Rise in North London. Housing

---

23 Details are given in the archived record *Especially*, by Kenneth Dix (2007), p.35.
24 *"Hitherto": A Short Account of the Aged Pilgrims' Friend Society 1807–1957*, p.37.

eighty pensioners, the new home was built at a cost of £12,000 and was situated on the edge of the countryside; so rapid was the sprawl of London that by 1907 it was described as 'an oasis amidst a wilderness of bricks and mortar.' The yellow brick Hornsey Rise home, situated opposite the newly built Alexandra Orphanage, was opened on 4 July 1871 by Arthur (later Lord) Kinnaird, with the son of the German Ambassador chairing. Set on higher ground in open country, the air was relatively fresh for a London suburb and the gardens in the centre of the square of homes were laid out with flowers and shrubs.

Laying the foundation stone of Hornsey Rise on 24 May 1870

The apartments were in two stories, but because the site was on a split level, connecting corridors avoided the need for stairs. Each resident had their own room with a recess for their bed and 'a coal cellar, scullery with running water, and shelves for domestic utensils'. They bought and cooked their own meals. Apart from the bed and mattress, which were

The Hornsey Rise Asylum

provided by the Society, residents were able to bring their own furniture with them including, in some cases, their own piano or a bird in a cage, although cats and dogs were not allowed. A 'pleasant little chapel', built in a Gothic style, meant that services could be held two or three times a week. The home also included the free use of a well-stocked library. Married couples were catered for as well.

The visitors' book of this home contained the names of many lords and ladies, including that of Lord Shaftesbury, and always they left comments of the homeliness and peacefulness of Hornsey Rise. The annual cost of maintaining a resident in the home, in addition to their pension, was estimated at this time, and for decades to come, to be around £7.12 shillings.[25]

It is hard to imagine a greater contrast between this Aged Pilgrims' Home, where the elderly, well fed and enjoying the comfort of their warm room with their personal items of nostalgia around them, were able to pursue their own interests and hobbies, with the miserable existence of the Workhouse inmates. One resident included in a letter to her friend: '… I have such a pleasant room; no landlady to hold the sword over you, and no rent to pay or coals to buy. I feel as I sit in my little freehold I must be praising my heavenly Father all day long, when I think of His love and kindness to me in the decline of life. I can say from my heart, not one of His promises has failed. He has promised me as my days so shall my strength be.'[26]

In 1876 a substantial gift by a friend of the Society was given anonymously (though later known to be John Benjamin Pope) to build an additional forty rooms and a large lecture hall capable of holding 300 people. This meant that the elderly residents were not entirely cut off from the outside world and could socialise with those who came for the various 'magic lantern' lectures. The Lady Visitors regularly brought in extra meals and meat for the residents and for many years a special Christmas dinner was provided.

---

25 The Society's collected and published *Quarterly Record* 1901–1905, p. 185.
26 John E Hazelton, *"Inasmuch": A History of the Aged Pilgrims' Friend Society 1807–1907* (London: Robert Banks & Son, 1907), p. 106.

For those who were no longer able to look after themselves, 'infirmary rooms' enabled them to receive nursing care. By 1881 there were 112 residents, three of whom were men. The home included accommodation for the warden and his wife, and five nurses were on hand to assist. These were each paid five shillings a week to provide full-time care for each of the six patients in the infirmary.

The Hornsey Rise home closed in 1973 after providing a safe shelter for elderly pilgrims for a little over one hundred years.

More Pilgrim Homes

In the later years of the 19th century a number of homes were given to the Society as legacies or during the lifetime of the benefactor. It was evidence that the valuable work of the Aged Pilgrims' Friend Society had captured the imagination and support of the Christian public well beyond the city of London. At a time when there were by now literally scores of vital evangelical charities working across the country, it was encouraging that the Society was gathering an increasing and wider support base. The gift of established buildings had the advantage of a home ready for occupancy at minimal cost to the Society; only much later did these buildings become a burden on the Society's resources to maintain them in an acceptable condition.

A freehold property at West Worthing, facing the sea, was given by Col. Angus Croll in 1878 to be used as a convalescent home. Unfortunately, neighbours of the property objected to this and so it was sold and the following year **Egremont Lodge, Brighton** was purchased. A convalescent home by the sea was an excellent idea in theory; however, it proved impractical. It could only be used in the summer months, and for many of the pensioners the fatigue of a long railway journey was too much. It was therefore decided to convert the home into a residence for seven pensioners. By this time a strong auxiliary was formed in Brighton and their annual sale of work in the Royal Pavilion significantly contributed towards the costs of this home. In addition, forty-nine 'out-pensioners' in the Brighton area were supported by the Society. This was an indication of the wider vision of the Aged Pilgrims' Friend Society to serve not only London but elderly Christians wherever they were in need. In 1928 the home was enlarged to accommodate a further eleven residents.

The home in Brighton, Sussex was purchased in 1879

Funds for a home for nine pensioners and a caretaker in **Stamford Hill, North London** were given to the Society by Sarah Ward aged eighty-five, and opened in November 1883. Now, each resident had two rooms and received ten guineas a year. Gas fires were not installed until 1961 and seven years later the whole home was upgraded. By the 1980s it was clearly past further modernising and the home was sold in 1986.

A new home in the countryside at **Gerrards Cross, Buckinghamshire** was given to the Society in September 1875 by Sir John Wallace Alexander. He was a committed Christian who had supported the Society for many years. The 'ten suites of apartments' were specifically available for those who had served in full-time Christian ministry; many of whom were still able to minister in the surrounding villages even after entering the home. In the light of this, it is perhaps all the more sad to report that relationships within the home were not always what they should have been. By the middle of the next century the house was in need of significant repairs; it had been listed as a building of architectural interest and this certainly limited development and in 1973 the home was abandoned.

In 1899 land was purchased for a new building to house six residents and a matron in **Arthur Road, Hyde Street, Winchester** to commemorate the diamond jubilee of Queen Victoria. For the first time a building in a more modern style of architecture is evident. Electric lights were installed in 1934 and water heaters a year later. Improvements in 1989 meant that each of the flats was provided with a kitchen, bathroom and its own front door. A communal lounge, laundry and warden's flat was added. Unfortunately, only ten years later it was recognised that the building was outdated and too small; what had been perfectly satisfactory four decades earlier no longer met modern requirements for the elderly and, after a century of service, the home was closed.

In 1891 ten almshouses in **Clarendon Park Road, Leicester** were given to the Society.

However, at this time it was still the small pension reaching the largest number of the most elderly pilgrims that had a greater impact than the residential homes.

*Your very faithfully
and affectionately in Christ
Joseph Irons*

Joseph Irons,
a strong supporter
of the Society and a
frequent preacher at
the annual meeting

*Your very truly
JH Evans*

James Harrington
Evans
who, until his death
in a carriage accident
in 1849, regularly
preached for the
Society

Rowland Hill,
one of the most
popular London
preachers, first
preached for the
Society as early as 1827

William Wilberforce
was a Vice President of
the Society from 1824
until his death in 1833

Lord Shaftesbury,
a strong supporter and
patron of The Aged
Pilgrims' Friend Society

5: Growing support

A s the reputation of the Society spread, support occasionally came from surprising directions. The first record of a 'tea party' to raise funds occurs in April 1827. A few young men had organised a tea party at a tavern in Regents Park to raise money for 'distressed manufacturers'. That success encouraged them to plan another in the summer, and this time in aid of the Aged Pilgrims' Friend Society. Concerned for the good name of the Society, the Committee asked two pertinent questions: were all the men involved 'serious men' and would any 'profane or worldly singers' be involved? Satisfactory answers were given and the Committee was assured that only approved men would be present. The Committee agreed and acknowledged 'it has now become a general practice to hold public meetings at Taverns and other public places for the benefit of most of the religious institutions.' In the event, a minister was present, it was an orderly party and the collection amounted to £25.10s. 6d.

The first collection for the Society after a sermon was preached on its behalf was at Gower Street Chapel and amounted to the significant sum of £20 9s 6d. On some occasions, not only cash went into the collection plates. In March 1832 the committee was presented with a silk handkerchief that had been placed in one of the offering plates—it was auctioned to a committee member for three shillings and sixpence!

It is not surprising that support for the Society took some time to gather momentum. It was not that there were many Christian charities in London at this time, or that the Christian community was far more interested in overseas mission and direct gospel outreach. In fact, most of the evangelical home charities and Christian overseas missions in the Victorian era had not yet been founded as early as 1807. The chief drawback was that this fledging society, bothering about a forgotten section of society in a city groaning with poverty and destitute children, was the initiative of a cluster of relatively unknown lay men and women who, worse still, were nonconformists. There was not a single Lord or Sir among them. The only military man at the first meeting of the Society was a young, and then unknown, officer who the following year embarked on a lengthy overseas assignment.

However, despite the initial reticence of many ministers in London, particularly from the established church, to align themselves with this new charity, there were some loyal church leaders who supported the mission in its early years.

Born in 1785, **James Harrington Evans** was educated at Wadham College, Oxford, and became a fellow in 1805. He was ordained into the Church of England but by 1815 his forthright preaching of the gospel forced him to secede and the following year he was appointed as the minister of John Street Baptist Chapel, Grays Inn Road, London. He was for many years a strong supporter of the work of the Society until his death in Scotland in a tragic carriage accident in 1849.

On Sunday, 24 March 1839 Evans was preaching for the Society from the text 'He that hath pity upon the poor lendeth unto the LORD; and that which he hath given will he pay him again' (Proverbs 19:17). During his sermon, he presented the account of some of those he had personally visited, including one elderly Christian of 90 years and her daughter, somewhere between ages 60 and 70, who had to sell everything they had 'except their very clothes', to keep themselves alive even in the depth of winter. He told also of an elderly Christian, almost 80 years of age who, when pressed hard on what he had had for dinner, took the minister to the fireplace 'and showed me some grey peas'. He could not even afford bread. Very occasionally someone would give him a little piece of bacon, and his prized possession was a small portion of butter that he had been slowly eating over the past three months.

By this time, in 1839, there were 92 pensioners receiving five guineas a year, 166 receiving four shillings a month, and two in the Workhouse who received two shillings. The total annual expenditure of the mission was now £1,600, but the income was £500 short of this. Unashamedly Evans prompted those in the congregation who could afford it to become annual subscribers. He applied his sermon closely: 'And now I leave the case with the Lord and your own consciences. I told you at the beginning, I plead not for them, but I plead for the cause of Christ.' Evans had always argued against the common mistake that 'if we take care of principles in religion, holy practice is sure to follow'; he knew that holy practice did not always follow. He therefore presented a challenge to the congregation that if he could bring the elderly saints of whom he had been speaking into this chapel, there would be no question but that his hearers would give generously. However, he could not do this because few of them could even walk. Evans concluded, 'is *feeling*—or is *principle*—the moving course of our actions? Is it because my feelings are excited, or is it not the conviction of this truth, "Jesus, who was rich, for my sake became poor, that I through his poverty might be rich"'?

Joseph Irons was born at Ware in Hertfordshire in 1785. When he came to London he was a close friend of the converted slave-trader John Newton, but after Newton's death in 1802 Irons became a nonconformist and was wholly committed to the Westminster Confession of Faith; he once described himself as 'a Congregational Episcopalian'. He allowed no musical accompaniment to the hymn singing in his church. In 1818 Irons became pastor at the Grove Chapel, a Congregational Chapel in Camberwell. His powerful Calvinistic preaching, together with his hymns and poems, earned him a widespread reputation and his sermons were published in many countries across the world. Irons' character and preaching reflected his large and powerful frame—strong and unbending. His booming voice could be heard far outside the walls of the chapel. Robert Browning, the English poet who was born in Camberwell and rejected his mother's evangelical faith, would take his favourite Sunday walk with a friend past Grove Chapel; they played a game to see who could first hear the 'bawling' of Joseph Irons.

Irons remained a strong supporter of the Society and was the most frequent preacher at the annual meetings until his death in 1852. The first Auxiliary of the Society, the Camberwell Auxiliary, was established at Grove Chapel in 1835.

Rowland Hill was born in Shropshire in 1744, educated at Eton and Cambridge and, having been denied ordination by six bishops because of his evangelistic open-air preaching, he entered the independent ministry. An inheritance on the death of his father enabled him to build Surrey Chapel in Blackfriars Road, Southwark, and he became possibly the most popular preacher in London until his death in 1833. Rowland Hill was chairman of the Religious Tract Society and a strong supporter of the British and Foreign Bible Society and the London Missionary Society. A personal friend of Edward Jenner, the pioneer of the smallpox vaccination, he recommended it to all the congregations he preached to, long before it was medically accepted in England. Hill's support of the Aged Pilgrims' Friend Society was a great boost to their reputation and when he preached for the Society at Clapham in January 1827 the response was 'a very liberal collection' and four new subscribers.

William Wilberforce is known pre-eminently for his leading role in the abolition of slavery. It was a Sunday in 1787 that he famously wrote in his diary: 'God Almighty has placed before me two great objects. The suppression of the slave trade and the reformation of manners [morals].' That resolution effectively ended his rising political career.

Born in Hull in 1759 and educated at St John's College, Cambridge, Wilberforce had come under the influence of John Newton and his old mentor Dr Isaac Milner. He became MP for Yorkshire at the age of 25 but two years later he had fully embraced the evangelical gospel. On 12 May 1789 Wilberforce delivered his first salvo against the slave trade which was recognised by the great statesman, Edmund Burke, as the finest speech Parliament had heard in modern times.

After a long struggle, and its share of bitter disappointments and betrayals, on 23 February 1807 the bill abolishing the slave trade was eventually passed, noted by the prominent historian George M Trevelyan as 'one of the turning events in the history of the world'. This was also the year of the formation of the Aged Pilgrims' Friend Society. The Society was among the many charities supported by Wilberforce. He was a Vice President from 1824 until his death in 1833—the year in which the slaves throughout the British Empire were freed.

Lord Shaftesbury was born at 24 Grosvenor Square, London, six years before the Society was founded. He learned nothing of the Christian gospel from his parents: his mother was preoccupied with fashion houses and society, and his father with the affairs of state. It was a housekeeper,

Maria Millis, who taught him Bible stories and to whom he traced his first impressions of true Christian faith at the age of seven.

However, it was not until his 24th birthday that he could record in his diary: 'I have a great mind to found a policy on the Bible.' Towards the end of his life he could declare to his biographer: 'My religious views are not popular, but they are the views that have sustained and comforted me all through my life. They have never been disguised, nor have I ever sought to disguise them. ... I have always been—and, please God, always shall be—an Evangelical of the Evangelicals.'[27]

Like Wilberforce before him, Shaftesbury determined that the Bible would guide his course, and in consequence, like Wilberforce also, he gave up a promising political career to care for the downtrodden and outcasts of Victorian society. He committed himself to a Bill that eventually limited the hours of labour for women and children to ten hours a day, and he forced through measures to bring the children and women up from the mines, the little boys down from the chimneys and the orphans out from the gutter. His unceasing work on behalf of 'the poor lunatics in the asylums' has been called the Magna Carta for the liberties of the insane. His personal involvement in the suffering of almost every level of society, meant that when in 1841 he received an honorary doctorate from Oxford, he felt a cold distrust by the dons and students alike. He noted in his diary for June 15 of that year: 'I was received with courtesy and nothing more. My popularity, such as it is, lies with a portion of the great unwashed.'

It was hardly surprising therefore that he readily became a 'committed friend' of the Aged Pilgrims' Friend Society and chaired the annual meeting on four occasions, the first in 1855. Shaftesbury gladly chaired for many Christian institutions and during the annual May Meetings of 1872, when no fewer than sixty-nine societies held their annual meetings in London, he presided at sixteen, including the annual meeting of the Aged Pilgrims' Friend Society. On his last occasion in 1883, just two years before his death, he commented of the Society:

---

27 Edwin Hodder, *The Life and Work of the Seventh Earl of Shaftesbury* (London: Cassell and Company Limited, 1892), pp. iv-v.

'This Institution, apart from the benefit and relief it gives, is a great moral Institution, and is set to create in men's hearts and minds a feeling of reverence which is necessary in things moral, political and religious. Old people are apt to be regarded as a burden. For this reason, I specially commend the Charity to young people.'

The wisdom of this last statement was reinforced by a comment in the report of the first hundred years of the Society in 1907: 'It would do our young pilgrims good, as a part of a sound Christian education, if they would now and then go and see old Pilgrims, and hear them bear their testimony of Jesus.'[28]

Other strong supporters of the Society in the early years included such diverse religious leaders as **William Gadsby**, the Strict and Particular Baptist pastor and hymn writer, **Alfred Hewlett**, the vicar at Astley near Manchester, who always preached for the Society when he was in London, and the outspoken evangelical **Hugh M'Neile**, the Dean of Ripon. **Dr David Doudney**, the warm-hearted vicar of St Luke's, Bedminster, Bristol, who for over half a century edited *The Gospel Magazine* and produced the small tract, *Words for the Weary and Worn; to the inmates of the Aged Pilgrims' Friend Society's Asylums*, was a regular visitor at the Hornsey Rise home. In 1884 he preached for the Society from the pulpit once occupied by John Newton at St Mary Woolnoth in the City of London; a large congregation gathered and the collection was in excess of £100. **Lord Kinnaird**, an influential politician and benefactor of many Christian charities, and **Lord Justice Lush**, who later became Lord Justice of Appeal, were among many who regularly supported the Society.

In 1884 **Horatius Bonar**, a Church of Scotland minister and later a founder of the Free Church of Scotland, composed a hymn especially for the Society. A popular writer in his day, producing a book almost every year, he is better known for his hymns of which he composed some 600 and was known as the 'Prince of Scottish hymn writers'. The hymn he composed for the Society is one of his very few in which we know precisely when and why he wrote it which, under the title 'But thou art rich', was based on Revelation 2:9 and consisted of nine verses. (See Appendix B here).

---

28 John E Hazelton, *"Inasmuch": A History of the Aged Pilgrims' Friend Society 1807-1907*, p. 175.

The leaflet announcing a meeting at the Metropolitan Tabernacle, London in 1888 at which Spurgeon would preach on behalf of the Aged Pilgrims' Friend Society. It was his last sermon for the Society before his death in January 1892.

The Baptist pastor, **C H Spurgeon**, first preached for the Society on Thursday evening 25 September 1856, at the age of 22 years, in his chapel in New Park Street, Southwark under the title 'The duty of remembering the poor'[29] and he remained a firm friend and supporter until his death in 1892.

A portrait of Charles Haddon Spurgeon age 36

An outline of Spurgeon's sermon on behalf of the Aged Pilgrims' Friend Society in September 1856

Spurgeon introduced his subject based on Galatians 2:10 'Only that we should remember the poor; the same which I also was forward to do.' He referred to the fact that grace is more frequently found in poverty than in riches. The 'prince of preachers', as he has become known, then outlined his three headings: The fact that God has a poor people, the duty that we should remember the poor, and finally the obligation for us to perform this duty.

---

29 Sermon no. 99 in the Metropolitan Pulpit. It was first published the Penny Pulpit series No. 2,660.

Under his first heading, Spurgeon was sufficiently bold to tackle the question why God should allow poverty. He had a six-point answer: poverty should make those of us who are not so afflicted more grateful for our comforts, it is a demonstration of God's sovereignty to dispense prosperity as he wills among his own people, poverty highlights the value of the comforts of the promises of God in his word, it is a 'plague to the devil' that so many poor Christians remain faithful to their God, poverty helps us to understand a little of the poverty of our Saviour, and poverty provides the opportunity to express the generous heart of Christian people.

For his second heading Spurgeon reminded his hearers that they should remember the poor in our *prayer*: 'Let the angel touch you on the arm, when you have nearly finished your prayer, and say, "Remember the poor; remember the poor of the flock."' In our *conversation*: we are always ready to talk about the rich and respectable and influential, but there is no command in Scripture to remember the rich; however, there is a command to remember the poor. We have all the time in the world to stop and greet the rich, but too often we cannot find a moment to greet the poor. We must remember them also in our *provision for their necessities*. The preacher commented that he can never forget them because 'I have about ten times as many poor people come to me every day as I can possibly relieve… How many of our lavish luxuries might be bestowed on that which they crave for their very existence.'

Finally, Spurgeon urged his congregation to remember the poor, not on the ground of 'philanthropy and charity', but because they are the Lord's brethren. We show that we love Christ only when we love his people, and we may lose our wealth by the misuse of it.

Spurgeon closed by commending the Aged Pilgrims' Friend Society 'as an especially excellent institution, because it will enable you to remember the poor'. All the recipients are Christians 'as far as man can judge', they are supported by wise Christian stewards of the funds, and 'last of all they are all over sixty.' Spurgeon then read part of the Society's report for that year which closed with a reference to the value of legacies. In typical Spurgeonic style, and we can imagine with a twinkle in his eye, he commented: 'Our friends had no business to say anything about legacies, for we do not wish you to die just yet; we always wish to have your subscriptions. We are very thankful to receive legacies, but do not keep the money to leave us in the shape of legacies. We would rather have your annual subscriptions for ten years; for then we should have your living prayers, your living sympathy, and your living help. Well, if you do not think this is a good society, do not give anything; but if you do, just put it on its merits … and give as you think the society deserves to receive, and as you believe yourselves able to bestow. May God give a blessing to you in remembering the poor.'

Steady growth

The first three decades of the Society saw a firm growth both in the number of supporters and the pensioners. The annual report of the committee (which now comprised twenty-four members) for 1838 could list donations from sixty-five Life Members (those who had initially subscribed twenty guineas) and from almost 900 Annual Subscribers of one guinea or more. In addition, almost £3,000 in legacies and a further £1,000 in occasional donations had been received during the year. However, this was the year in which the first residential home had been opened and some of the donations and legacies would reflect this.

This 'truly gratifying Report' of 1838 provided the names, addresses and ages of 50 pensioners who received ten guineas per annum (the eldest being ninety-eight and the youngest sixty-seven), 111 receiving five guineas per annum, 120 'Approved Candidates' receiving four shillings a month

Surrey Gardens Music Hall where the Rev James Wells preached for the Society to a congregation of 10,000 in 1858

and one in the workhouse receiving two shillings a month. In all, over 270 Pilgrims were supported by the Society in this year; 42 of these were living in the new home at Camberwell. By 1871 there were 703 pensioners costing an annual expenditure of £3,884. It was also particularly noted that expenses were kept to a minimum because both the Secretary and the Treasurer offered their services freely.

Evidence for the increasing reputation of the Society is seen in the fact that at the Annual Meeting held at the City of London Tavern in April 1838, Sir Cullen Eardley Smith, a strong advocate for Christian unity and overseas missions, was in the chair. As the century progressed, this became even more evident. In 1858 when the Rev. James Wells of the Surrey Tabernacle preached for the Society in the Surrey Gardens Music Hall, it was estimated that 10,000 were in the congregation to hear him preach from Galatians 5:6 'faith which worketh by love'. When, in 1884, Dr David Doudney preached for the Society in John Newton's church at St Mary Woolnoth in the City of London, the church had to be closed twenty minutes before the commencement of the service and people crammed the aisles.

To maintain the non-denominational position of the Society, it was agreed that the chair at the Annual Meeting would never be taken by a minister of religion. Instead, invitations were given to politicians like Lord Shaftesbury, military men such as General Sir William Stirling, and

Exeter Hall, built specifically for the use of religious and other societies, was opened on 29 March 1831 to seat 4,000 in the main auditorium. It was demolished in 1907 and the Strand Palace Hotel occupies its site

others of significant influence in the City, including Sir John Thwaites who was chairman of the Metropolitan Board of Works and a member of the Aged Pilgrims' Friend Society Committee from 1851 until his death in 1870. From 1831 the Lord Mayor of the City of London was ready to take the chair for the Society at its annual meeting held in the newly opened Exeter Hall.

These meetings were well attended throughout the latter part of the 19th century by ministers and lay people representing a wide spectrum of evangelical life from the Church of England to Baptists and a variety of Independents.

A paid Secretary

With the steady growth of the Society, the work taken on by both the Secretary, John Box, and the Treasurer, Thomas Carmen, became almost too much. By 1835 both felt that they would have to resign, although in the event they continued. The suggestion that the secretary should be paid for his work was discussed and rejected because it was always the desire of the Society that everyone involved should do so in an honorary capacity. This was a laudable principle that would eventually prove impossible to maintain.

In April 1859 James Bisset, the founding member and driving force of the Society for half a century, died; John Box followed him three years later. These two had shared the position of Honorary Secretary for more than thirty years. It now became obvious that with the pressure of mounting responsibilities with over 500 pensioners, 40 residents, a rapidly increasing number of Auxiliaries and an ever-widening reputation across the country, the position of a paid Secretary was essential.

In January 1863 Michael Murphy was appointed as the full-time secretary at a salary of £150 per annum. At the same time the Society rented an office in the City at number 10 Poultry. Murphy proved to be a very capable and diligent secretary whose 'ability, kindliness and high Christian character had done much to promote the welfare' of the

Society. He held his post until his death seventeen years later when he was described as 'unanimously beloved'.

The Annual Meeting held in Exeter Hall on 20 May 1878 was certainly not the happiest in the history of the Society but it may have been the most far-reaching in its effects. It had been preceded by significant disunity among the Hornsey Rise Lady Visitors. The Society had always tried to maintain an open stance both in its representation on the main Committee and among its pensioners and residents. However, it was evident that some thought differently, and nominations for Committee members who came from a wider group of churches was decidedly blocked by those who held a strongly Calvinistic position. For a while, therefore, the Society limited its appeal to a wider Christian public.[30]

On the death of Michael Murphy in 1880, John Hazelton became Secretary of the Society. Although only twenty-six years old when he took on the post, he served the Society with efficiency and enthusiasm for many years. However, in 1896 he had also taken on the pastorate of the Strict Baptist Chapel in Marylebone. The membership of over 300 and the strain of both ministries was beginning to tell. John Hazelton prepared the history of the Society for its Centenary in 1907[31] at which time, after twenty-seven years of faithful service, he was warmly thanked for all that he had done and received many interesting gifts including an electric kettle.

---

30 A detailed account of this unhappy meeting is given in the archived *Especially*, pp. 56-59.
31 John E Hazelton, *"Inasmuch": A History of the Aged Pilgrims' Friend Society 1807–1907* (London: Robert Banks & Son, 1907).

*In 1885 the Society held its annual meeting for the first time in the
Mansion House in the City of London*

6. A new century

In the first two decades of the 20th century British military power controlled almost a quarter of the land area of planet earth and one fifth of its population. London was the largest and most wealthy city in Europe and the controlling capital of the largest and most valuable empire known to human history. But the divide between rich and poor had changed only at the margins. Whilst vast resources poured into this financial centre of the 'civilised' world, the poverty of the slums remained a tragic and disgraceful blot in the heart of the city.

Worse still, just as in the 18th century people would pay to visit Bedlam on a Sunday afternoon to have tea with the inmates and 'enjoy' their ridiculous antics, so it became fashionable towards the end of the 19th century for the wealthy to visit the slums simply for the pleasure of observing the life of those they barely knew existed. This 'urban tourism' was known as 'slumming'. In 1884 the *New York Times* reported that slumming had even spread to the American capital.

On the back of this sordid pleasure, it was also popular for fashionable men and women to visit the many institutions of charity, mostly Christian, caring for the poor and destitute of London's slums. By the 1890s London guidebooks not only directed visitors to shops, monuments, and churches but also mapped excursions to well-known philanthropic institutions located in notorious slum districts such as Whitechapel and Shoreditch.

Shameful though this guilty pleasure in observing the poor was, it at least brought to the attention of the wealthy not only the chronic state of the slums, but the fact that there were countless Christian charities caring for those in such distressed circumstances.

A mission still urgently needed

It was perhaps a mark of the Aged Pilgrims' Friend Society coming of age when in October 1885 a meeting was held for the first time in the Mansion

House in the city of London. From 1894 the Annual Meeting was held in the Egyptian Hall with the blessing of the Lord Mayor and with many dignitaries present.

By the turn of the century the Committee, which had numbered thirteen in 1807 and twenty-four in 1838, had now risen to twenty-eight. From twenty-two Lady Visitors in 1838 there were now thirty-four. When the 20th century dawned, 1,529 pensioners from all over the country were being supported and the annual expenditure was above £11,600 for pensions and £2,000 for the homes. 218 pensioners were now receiving seven guineas a year instead of five.

As the work of the Society spread across the country, 'deputation' meetings were offered to raise awareness of and funds for the work. The *Quarterly Record* for July 1901 advertised: 'A lecture upon the Aged Pilgrims' Friend Society; its history and its friends, illustrated by seventy limelight views can be given during the autumn and winter season, in any part of the country.' The Society was using modern technology to spread its valuable work. Even at this time, when the Society was becoming well known and highly respected, the chairman of the annual meeting in 1901 commented that it was engaged in a work that was 'necessary and urgent, yet apt to be overlooked or forgotten'. Mr Justice Bruce continued that so much attention is paid to children, and rightly so: 'But when life is spent, when strength has gone and the faculties are failing, and the aged are poor and destitute, there is often little interest about their condition.'[32] Unfortunately, that message has often not changed today.

What also had not changed in the changing times, was the basis upon which the Society aided those in need. In July 1902, the Rev J H Hallet of Brighton, speaking at a quarterly meeting, emphasised three salient conditions for those who would receive the Society's help: they must be elderly (which then meant over sixty years of age), poor and godly. This latter point was unashamedly held by the Society from the very beginning, and for many years the emphasis that it was a Protestant Society was not lost. Whilst recognising the need to do good to all, it was the special

---

32 The Society's collected and published *Quarterly Record*, 1901-1905, 15 July 1901, p. 22.

duty of the Society to care for those who had a sincere and tested faith in Christ. One speaker questioned, 'How can you define a true Christian?' and followed with his own answer: 'True Christians betray themselves by their love for Jesus Christ, by the peace of God filling their hearts, and the blessed hope of heaven lighting up their faces.'[33] Nothing had changed in this regard since C H Spurgeon preached his sermon for the Society in 1858.

Other speakers in these years emphasised the fact that whilst many Christian institutions with very laudable purposes had come and gone, the Aged Pilgrims' Friend Society had maintained a growing and unswerving commitment to its initial cause for, at that time, almost a full century. One speaker in July 1902 offered the prophetic comment: 'The Society is destined to grow.' It is equally encouraging to read General Sir W Stirling commenting that a financier had passed to him the judgement that 'of all charitable institutions this Society was one of the most economically worked.'

At the annual meeting of the Society in 1902, the Rev F S Webster underlined the way in which a society is reflected by its care for the elderly; there was perhaps something prophetic about this also:

'I want most heartily to commend the Society, first of all, because it is a work amongst the aged. I have a very strong feeling that the respect which a community shows towards its aged members is a true test of its temper and spirit, and that a community where the aged are respected, is enlightened and stable, and that where the aged are not respected, that community is very fast going downhill ... The aged have a right to our reverence, and in need of our care... Are our aged Pilgrims to go off into the Workhouse? Is the Church to lose the benefit and blessing of their ripe experience, of their spiritual maturity, of their clearer vision of heavenly things, of their well tested confidence in Jesus Christ? ... I do not know a better use that could be made of the Lord's treasure than of helping the aged Pilgrims who are His.'[34]

However, two significant changes were noted by the Rev A J Baxter of Eastbourne at the annual meeting two years later. He commented that old age was beginning much sooner; at forty-five a man was often

---

33 As above and following pages.
34 As above, p.91 for January 15, 1903.

considered too old for a situation because younger men could be employed at a cheaper rate. In addition, he went on to comment that two shillings a week was becoming a far less valuable income than once it was; it would now buy a loaf of bread, some tea and butter, plus a little firewood and a few coals, but not much more. This led Baxter to suggest that the homes for the elderly are 'the brightest features in this institution'. Clearly he was a man who was both practical and visionary. That reference to the reduction in the purchasing value of the minimum pension was a matter constantly under review by the Committee, and would lead eventually to the abandoning of it altogether.

Baxter was also outspoken. The picture of perfect harmony and peace in the homes is reiterated time and again in the *Quarterly Record* and 'a little heaven on earth' is frequently the image used. However, for the first time we are confronted with the reality by Baxter: 'I am told, by the way, that they are not all amiable people, and that they do not always agree.' He then added, and we can imagine with a mischievous grin: 'You may depend upon it that human nature is the same under the roof at Hornsey Rise, or Camberwell as it is anywhere else....' This honest and down to earth minister then admitted to his shame that there was no Auxiliary in his own town of Eastbourne, but closed his address with a strong commitment to the unchanging gospel of Christ in the face of the rise of 'error and formal religion', a commitment that he knew was shared by the Society.[35]

This annual meeting in 1904 must have been a challenging experience for all who were present. Not only did they listen to A J Baxter dispel the idea of every Pilgrim Home being a never-broken haven of Christian harmony and peace, but the Dean of Peterborough related the experience of a missionary from the shores of the Hudson Bay. This long serving missionary described what frequently happened when an old Indian hunter was no longer able to keep up with the younger men and he was of no use to the tribe: 'When he lies down in his tent at night, perhaps very weary, there comes one behind him with a bow string, and that bow string is fastened

---

35 As above, p. 163 for July 15, 1904.

The Quarterly Record, *1892, 1916, 1937, 2015 indicating the changing styles of covers*

round his neck and he is quietly strangled.' The Dean contrasted this with the aged pilgrims who, although their contribution to the economy was 'infinitesimally small', yet 'there is something they can do, from a Christian point of view. Their example will tell. They are the servants of the Most High God'. The Dean continued that it is our duty to make them as happy and comfortable as possible because they are, 'a valuable section of the Church of Christ on earth. We cannot do without them. Their counsel, their patience, and their spirit of submission to God are important factors in the life of the Church of Christ. Do not think that you are conferring all the benefit … They are conferring also a benefit upon all around them.' In contrast to the tragic end of the aged Indian, this was proof of the power of Christ, and thus the Society, was based not simply on the principles of philanthropy but on the love of God in the heart. The Dean concluded by reminding the supporters in 1904 that prayer for the mission was the most valuable contribution that anyone could make.[36]

1907 was not only the centenary year of the Society, but it was also the year in which William Lever, the founder of Port Sunlight and the Lever (Unilever) empire, introduced into Parliament the idea of a state Old Age Pension paid through the post office. In this year there were 1,631 Aged Pilgrims' Friend Society pensioners from the Shetland Islands to Cornwall and from Ireland to East Anglia at the cost of £12,000 a year; the support of the various Pilgrim Homes amounted to £43 every day. The State Old Age Pension for the estimated 650,000 eligible men was not implemented until two years later and those qualifying—and there were severe restrictions on income and character—were paid five shillings a week. By comparison, back in 1838 the Society had increased their pension for some Pilgrims to ten guineas per annum, which meant they were even then paying just over four shillings a week.

Letters of appreciation reached the committee of the Society continually. One pensioner in 1903 wrote to express gratitude from the Shetland Isles. Suffering significantly himself, he commented that he left his 'poor old dying wife and sister entirely in the hands of our heavenly Father' and added

---

36 As above, p. 167.

appreciatively: 'The pension has helped us to live and keep together, so that though old and feeble, we are happy. Soon, through the blood of Calvary, we shall be where there is no pain and sorrow, and until then I would lean on Jesus.'

A group of Aged Pilgrims at Hastings early in the 20th century

Staying together was a vital part of the enabling of the small pension. The terrible fear of many frail, elderly couples was that they might have to end up in the dismal Workhouse where they would be separated and never again live together. This 'staying together' and keeping out of the 'House' or the 'Poor House', as the Workhouse was often referred to, was of first importance for all elderly Christian Pilgrims. A report in 1907 commented that the pensioners were 'the most deserving and the least assertive.'

Pensioners at Hornsey Rise early in the 20th century

There is little doubt that the pensions received by the Society and the homes in which many were enabled to spend their closing years certainly added to their longevity. In the year of the Society's centenary it was reported that of the 1,641 pensioners, 836 were in their 70s, 390 in their 80s and 33 more than 90 years old!

Chapter 6

A snapshot of the Society in 1910 [37]

The 103rd annual meeting for the year ending 31 March 1910 was held in the Cannon Street Hotel on Friday evening, 6 May 1910. The published report opened with that appropriate quotation from the seventh Earl of Shaftesbury at an annual meeting in the previous century quoted earlier:

'This Institution, apart from the benefit and relief it gives, is a great moral Institution, and is set to create in men's hearts and minds a feeling of reverence which is necessary in things moral, political, and religious. Old people are apt to be regarded as burdens, whereas it should be a joy and a privilege to minister to them. For this reason, I specifically commend the Charity to young people.'

The report acknowledged that the government's Old Age Pensions Act (1908) had been in operation for just one year and this may have challenged the need for the Society to continue paying pensions. Of the 1,646 pilgrims receiving a pension from the Society at a total cost of £12,189 per annum, 790 were also in receipt of the State Old Age Pension and most of them at the full rate of five shilling weekly. However, once the cost of the 200 in the four Pilgrim Homes had been taken into account, the additional income allowed for little more than help in meeting special demands, such as day and night attendance for those who were particularly fragile. By this time there were three categories of Pilgrims' annual pensions: ten, seven and five guineas.

The past year had been hard for the Society because 'the times are difficult financially'. Donations were slightly less than in the previous year although the support for the work was still strong across the country. Legacies had increased during the year, although even this was reflective of a loss of many supporters through death. Every effort was being made to keep administration costs as low as possible and currently they ran at around eight percent of income. [38]

---

37 *The Aged Pilgrims' Friend Society 1910* (published by the Society at 83 Finsbury Pavement, London EC).

38 Even today that would be considered a remarkably low percentage for the operating cost of a Christian mission.

Sales of work were still effective in providing new income, the Lady Visitors continued to make a valuable contribution to the comfort and wellbeing of the pensioners, and the twenty-three Auxiliaries were vital to the progress of the Society. Apart from the long tradition of sermons preached on behalf of the Society, it appears from the report that many informal meetings in homes and elsewhere were held for the work.

The system of voting for the Accepted Candidates who could now qualify for a pension remained unchanged from the beginning. All paid-up subscribers were entitled to vote and the report in 1910 was careful to outline the procedure which ensured that every effort was made for it to be fair and transparent. This system may seem strange to a modern reader but it served the Society well and was, in fact, a condition of some supporters continuing with their subscription; one specifically writing that he would continue with his two guinea annual subscription 'as long as they have open voting'. It at least had the merit that no one could accuse the committee of favouring their own candidates.

Of the current pensioners in 1910, 533 were single, 179 married and 934 were widows. 36 were over ninety years of age. Only 207 pensioners were men, which was thirteen percent of the total. During the year 185 pensioners 'have said farewell to this world'.

The report stressed that after more than a century, the ethos and principles of the Society had not changed, and a commitment to the 'perfection and completeness of the revelation given by God

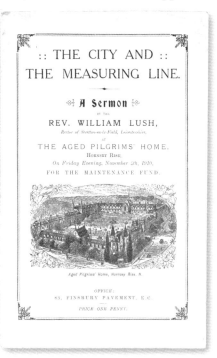

:: THE CITY AND ::
THE MEASURING LINE.

A Sermon
BY THE
REV. WILLIAM LUSH,
Rector of Stretton-on-le-Field, Leicestershire,
AT
THE AGED PILGRIMS' HOME,
Hornsey Rise,
On Friday Evening, November 4th, 1910,
FOR THE MAINTENANCE FUND.

Aged Pilgrims' Home, Hornsey Rise, N.

OFFICE:
83, FINSBURY PAVEMENT, E.C.

PRICE ONE PENNY.

The cover of the sermon preached by the Rev. William Lush for the Society in November 1910

in His verbally inspired Word and in their adherence to the distinctive truths of vital religion as expressed in the Trust Deeds and prefixed to the published Report' was as strong as ever. Like all the annual reports, this one from 1910 was rooted in references to Scripture as the basis for their work. The Aged Pilgrims' Friend Society should never be seen merely as another charitable institution, but always as a caring Society embedded in a commitment to the authority and commands of Scripture. That had been undeniably the case for the first one hundred years, and nothing changed as it entered the second.

The report of 1910 included a few cameos of elderly pensioners. Here are just three:

A pensioner, aged 75, from Lincolnshire: 'is a great sufferer; she needs many little extras, milk etc which will cost money. Her husband is often unable to work for weeks together. I do not know what they would do without the pension. It relieves them from laying aside for the rent. Her neighbours are kind, but they cannot be expected to do all her work for nothing. She, poor woman, can hardly do anything; often not able to stand, and her hands so crippled that she can only feed herself with difficulty.'

A pensioner, aged 70, from Gloucestershire: 'I am thankful for the pension; the Committee little know how the burden of the future has been lifted from my remaining days; for the pension pays my rent, and now I cannot see to earn much by my needle; it is a great boon, for it enables me to keep my home together.'

A pensioner who died in her 86th year on the Isle of Wight: 'For more than five years she was bedridden and used to say there was one thing she could do, and that was to carry the other aged Pilgrims and others constantly before the Throne of Grace. She could repeat nearly 200 of the good old Gospel hymns, and had a wonderful memory for Holy Scripture. Her hope was based absolutely upon Christ and His finished work. "O receive my soul at last" she said, and soon after passed away.'

A report on the four homes of the Society noted that the cost of keeping each resident amounted to less than the three shillings and sixpence a week they would have to pay for equivalent accommodation outside; in addition, they were supplied with 'coals, medical attendance, and other comforts', and had the benefit of the regular fellowship of the Lady

Visitors. Restrictions were kept as few as possible 'consistent with proper order'. Perhaps a little of the long-established habit of society in general viewing those in need was still prevalent when the subscribers were invited to visit the homes and meet the residents to experience the 'welcoming smile our aged friends extend to visitors'.

Camberwell, after three-quarters of a century, was still happily occupied by forty-two residents. The home at Hornsey Rise which, fifty-three years earlier, had been built in the country 'overlooking the huge metropolis that lay basking at your feet' was by now 'swallowed up by the ever-advancing city itself', but it was still a place for 'peace, comfort and health'. The home that was built for eighty residents had been extended and now provided a residence for one hundred and twenty. Stamford Hill in north London could be 'easily reached by train or tram, but is out of the noise of traffic'; here each resident or married couple enjoyed two rooms. The home in Brighton housed seven residents and fifty-one in the town received pensions. It is hardly surprising therefore that the report commented on the county of Sussex providing 'some of our heartiest supporters'.

The work of the Lady Visitors was especially appreciated. Their valuable contribution included paying the pensions, organising sales of work, overseeing the collection and distribution of the Benevolent Fund for the homes and regularly visiting the elderly residents.

The detailed report for 1910 had been published beforehand and included a full statement of the Society's finances, its thirty-four Rules and Regulations, plus another thirty-one for the Homes and seven for the Benevolent Funds. This was followed by the names and addresses of all subscribers—well in excess of 2,500—and how much they subscribed, details of the churches and chapels that donated, the Auxiliaries, and names and addresses of all pensioners and residents in the Pilgrim Homes. The careful records and openness of the Society from the very beginning avoided any accusation of wasteful spending or misappropriation of funds.

By this year 1910, 8,620 Pilgrims had received pensions at a total cost of £412,000.

The annual meeting that accepted this report closed, as was customary, with the doxology and the benediction.

The Committee of the Society in 1907

7. Progress in change

If the Edwardian era, from 1901 to 1910, was a time of economic prosperity for many, few could anticipate the immense changes that would take place before the second decade of the century came to an end. The City of London continued to be the financial centre of the world, and the British Empire, for a while, still provided vast wealth for the 'mother country'. However, 1914 changed everything.

In the middle of the war, the annual report for 1916 commented solemnly: 'The awful conflict in which we are now engaged has profoundly affected the whole country, from the largest centre down to the remotest village, and the work of the Society—like everything else—has been considerably interfered with in many ways.' However, on a brighter note, attendance at meetings and collections had been 'up to the average … sometimes even better than usual'. Focusing on the desperate need of the time, the report continued: 'The worldwide War causes great searchings of heart, and the people of God pray that to the nation it may be said "hear ye the rod, and Who hath appointed it," and that the outcome may be a national turning unto God, the recognition of the Bible as the verbally inspired Word, the keeping of the Lord's Day, and the forsaking of superstition, heresies, and the love of pleasure.'

A year later the news was not encouraging: 'The Legacies are below the average of the past decade; if this diminution continues, the Pension expenditure will be materially affected. Already, owing to the non-payment of Bequests, through the War, loans have had to be obtained from our Bankers, and the Committee strongly feel that no debt ought to be incurred for the Lord's work.'

As the war drew to its close in 1918, the Rev. Ernest Row of Surrey Chapel commented in his sermon for the Society: 'The past year has made immense demands on Christian faith and fortitude. We look back across months of strain, anxiety, and grief. Our vision of things to come is blurred with blood and fire and vapour of smoke … Yet among heart-shattering changes we find refuge in those things which cannot be shaken and remain ... Though the axis of earth may seem to have shifted, the changeless pole-star of the Everlasting Gospel shines for all the scattered and sorrowful people of God.'

The laudable purpose of the government to build one million new council houses at the close of the Great War to replace some of the worst slums, was partly offset by an inevitable increase in rents. Although the worst of the poverty of the previous century was to a degree overcome, still the Society pension made all the difference between many pilgrims being able to pay their rent or running into great debt.

For the Society, the year 1919 was significant not only as the first full year of peace after the Great War, but because the pension for the pilgrims was raised to 25 shillings a month. This was a considerable increase and, as one resident expressed it in a letter of appreciation: 'It has made a pair of warm boots possible. So badly needed, yet seemingly out of reach.' At the same time the voting system which, for all its good intentions had been open to 'manipulation', was discontinued and pensions were given to Approved Candidates on the nomination of contributors, and admission to the Pilgrim Homes was now in the order of application and approval—something the ladies had recommended decades earlier!

Sales of work continued, and whilst the Society always avoided the typical fundraising bazaar, they recognised the value that some, who could not give much in money, were able to 'employ their talents in procuring money'. As always with the Society, a biblical

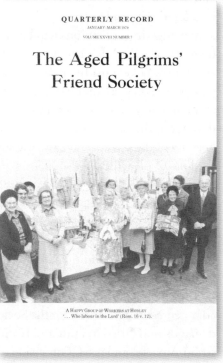

QUARTERLY RECORD
JANUARY-MARCH 1979
VOLUME XXVIII NUMBER 7

The Aged Pilgrims'
Friend Society

A HAPPY GROUP OF WORKERS AT HORLEY
'... Who labour in the Lord' (Rom. 16 v. 12).

A sale of work at Horley in 1979

precedent was applied, this time in the provision for the Tabernacle, where some gave gold and silver and others the labour of their hands. In 1922 a specific appeal was made to young people to maintain the work which had been commenced by young people 115 years earlier: 'We look to you, thank God that an increasing number of your own generation are engaged in this service.'[39] The residents and pensioners of the Society were described as: 'The most deserving and the least assertive.'

1922 was the year in which the British Broadcasting Company was established, and three years later a resident requested permission to install a crystal wireless set in their room. Permission was not granted and when, by 1931, no fewer than eight inmates were listening to a wireless, they were ordered to remove them immediately—perhaps reflecting the influence of Strict Baptist practice on the work of the Society.

New homes for old

In May 1924, the committee appointed James Flegg as General Secretary and he continued in this role until his death in 1938 at the age of 73. It was not an easy position to take up, not only because he was following in the footsteps of an excellent and long-serving predecessor, but because the country was still suffering the terrible effects of the Great War and was sliding steadily into an economic depression. Inflation during the war peaked at 25% in 1917 and then slumped to a -14% deflation in 1922; it had barely adjusted to zero two years later. Britain had used up virtually all its resources to pay for the conflict and was forced to borrow, mainly from the USA. The trades unions gathered momentum, women now entered the workforce as never before, and when three quarters of a million servicemen were killed on the battlefield, a proportionately large number of widows were left behind—often destitute. 1921 saw a serious depression and soon three million men were unemployed. The general strike of 1926 only added to the misery.

---

39 John E Hazelton, "Inasmuch": A History of the Aged Pilgrims' Friend Society 1807–1922 (London: C J Farncombe & Sons, 1922), pp. 158-159.

However, it was evident that the purchase of existing homes for the specific use of the elderly was not ideal. This would become even more so with the ever-increasing government regulations as the 20th century progressed. Two homes in Tunbridge Wells, generously given to the Society in 1920, were sold in favour of a purpose-built home. In 1950 the Society was given two and a quarter acres of land in the village of Evington near Leicester for a new home. The Auxiliary in Leicestershire had been continually active since the first ten homes were given to the Society in 1891 in Clarendon Park Road. By 1954 the first phase of a brand new purpose-built complex at Evington was opened. It consisted of eight small bungalows for six residents and four nursing cases with accommodation for a matron and assistant. At the opening, the Lord Mayor of Leicester paid a warm tribute to the valuable and necessary work of voluntary organisations like the Aged Pilgrims' Friend Society. By this time, over two hundred residents were enjoying the benefits of Society homes. These bungalows were demolished sixty years later in favour of the award-winning Pilgrim Gardens.

Significantly, a report of the Society's work in 1957 stressed that even with the greatly improved conditions of 'State Pensions and National Assistance' there was as much need for the work of the Society pensions as ever because: 'The Society has kept abreast of the times in its work among the poor of the Lord's people, and has adjusted its help and developed its work along such lines as it considered most beneficial to those whom it has ever sought to assist.'[40] This willingness and ability to adapt to changing social and cultural conditions had enabled the Society to remain relevant to the current needs more than two hundred years after its foundation.

Nursing care

For many years the Society had been concerned to provide for their pilgrims when they needed nursing care. The care and comfort of the homes meant that the residents were living longer and this meant that

---

40 *"Hitherto": A Short Account of the Aged Pilgrims' Friend Society, 150 years of work and witness, 1807-1957* (published by Head Office at Ludgate Hill, London), p. 22.

they became more fragile. The only alternative when they could no longer care for themselves was the Infirmary attached to the dreaded Workhouse. Here, they were not only divorced from the regular Bible ministry that was so appreciated, but they lived among those who shared none of the values and priorities, the certain hope and confidence, that the Pilgrim communities enjoyed. Later in the century, the elderly infirm had to be removed to the local General Hospital, and even when local authorities were obliged to provide homes for the elderly after the introduction of the National Health Service in 1948, there was rarely little more than a tolerated Sunday service served by a local church, and the atmosphere of these homes was far from positive for an elderly Christian.

In 1924 it was decided to add a nursing wing to the Hornsey Rise home. What became known as 'The John E Hazelton Memorial' (named after the earlier General Secretary of the Society) provided twenty-two beds in two wards and two single rooms for those needing special care. An official report by The Housing Centre commented that the Society: 'have been pioneers in medical care by equipping a small model hospital in connection with their largest almshouses on Hornsey Rise so that their pensioners are never removed from their friends at the end of their days.' [41]

Immediately prior to World War II, Lady Anne Treves, widow of the surgeon to Queen Alexandra and King Edward VII, left a significant legacy to the Society with the understanding that she would like the nursing services to be extended. Unfortunately, the war intervened and the plans to add nursing wings to the homes at Brighton and Tunbridge Wells had to be put on hold. However, in July 1948 a nursing wing was opened at Brighton with a ward for four beds and two single rooms. Three years later an extension to the home at Tunbridge Wells provided what was described as 'this ultra-modern building—cheerful, airy, and full of light'. The large ward of twelve beds was complemented by single rooms and accommodation for the matron and her staff. This brought the Society's total of nursing care beds to sixty.

---

41 *The London Almshouses—six centuries of housing for the aged* (published by The Housing Centre, London, c. 1944), p. 7.

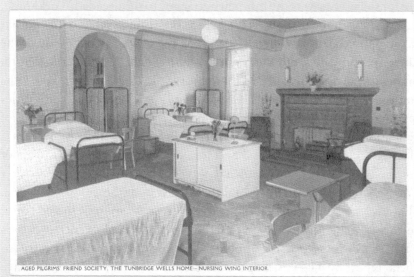

AGED PILGRIMS' FRIEND SOCIETY, THE TUNBRIDGE WELLS HOME—NURSING WING INTERIOR.

AGED PILGRIMS' FRIEND SOCIETY, THE TUNBRIDGE WELLS HOME AND NURSING WING, CAMBRIDGE GARDENS.

The Nursing care wing at Tunbridge Wells, Kent, opened in 1951

In September 1951, an additional six beds were constructed at Hornsey Rise. Sir Thomas Inskip, joint treasurer of the Society and later Lord Chancellor and Lord Chief Justice of England, laid the foundation stone and chaired the opening service. A nursing wing was added to the home in Evington in 1958 and extended in 1965, though later the extension was converted into residential care.

In those days, Christian charitable work was appreciated by the nation generally and a reporter from the *Leicester Evening Mail* could comment that he had seen:

'The ideal approach to the problems of old age. For this latest extension to the scheme at Evington is a "home" in the truest sense of the word. The word "home" should stand for comfort and security, beauty and peace. It should be a place where one can remain not only in health but also in sickness; somewhere, above all, that is not cut off from the stream of life, but is in community. Here, we have all of this.'[42]

Post war

When war with Germany again broke out in 1939 there were just over one thousand pensioners, but a year later it dropped to its lowest number for over half a century. With the steady rise in the state pension and the general uplift of wealth across the country, the Society pension gradually formed a less essential support for aged Christians. For those unable to receive a state pension, the Society increased its own pension to £24 per annum.

In preparation for the enemy bombing of London, air raid shelters were built to provide protection for the 170 residents in London homes. Mercifully, they were never needed and minimal damage was done to any of the homes. As might be expected, however, the income of the Society suffered during the war years yet, inevitably, with the destruction of so many houses in London the need for accommodation for ageing Christians was greater than ever. Reflecting the plight of neglected elderly Christians

---

42 Quoted in *Evidence*, p. 105.

at the commencement of the Society's work almost a century and a half earlier, the annual report of 1945 commented that with the desperate need of houses for families: 'The claims of aged people, are increasingly being pushed on one side by the exigencies of the period.' The report concluded that the need for the pension scheme had been overtaken by the need for accommodation.

With the continuing of rationing and the rising cost of living long after the close of the war, the pension was still a valuable support for many. This began to change with the end of all rationing in 1954 after fourteen long and meagre years. On the 150th anniversary of the Society in 1957 the report commented that in spite of 'State Pensions, supplementary allowances, and Public Assistance' the life pensions were still 'very necessary and greatly valued'. However, two years later there were only 58 pilgrims applying for a pension. At this time there were two hundred residents supported by thirty-three Auxiliaries across the country. With the significant rise in standards of living from the 1960s onwards, the number of pensioners would steadily decline.

Some indication of the growth of the Society in its first 150 years can be measured by its expenditure. In 1807 just over five pounds was expended on pensions, by 1957 with both pensions and residential homes it was approaching £30,000 and ten years later it reached £57,000.

By now many of the Society's homes were becoming increasingly expensive to maintain; in particular, Camberwell was certainly showing signs of ageing after 113 years, and the homes at Stamford Hill and Hornsey Rise were in the same condition—out of date with the advancing times and expectations and in serious need of costly renovation. Hornsey Rise soon found itself in a smokeless zone and the cost of converting all its coal fires to gas was cripplingly expensive; there was no electricity to the flats and the stone floors in the corridors were both noisy and cold. In spite of this, the report in 1957 still considered it 'vastly preferable to the top attics and damp basements in which many old people, unable to find anything better, have to be content to spend their days'. This was certainly true, but the Society's accommodation was clearly falling behind the rising standards and demands of the day.

In 1973 Hornsey Rise was sold and some of the remaining pilgrims were transferred to the new home at Wellsborough. The homes at Stamford Hill and Gerrards Cross had to be closed also. Major renovation took place at the Camberwell home in 1960, including central heating and plumbing to all the rooms. However, thirty years later further modernisation was urgently needed and, in 1991 after it had outlived six sovereigns and two World Wars in its 154-year history, the home at Camberwell was closed and sold.

In March 1960 a new General Secretary, Frank Clifford, was appointed, and on his retirement in 1973 George Reid took his place, followed in 1980 by Reginald Stewart.

Things unchanged but changing

The strong evangelical foundation of the work of the Aged Pilgrims' Friend Society has never changed since its inception. When the Secretary of the Society, John Hazelton, concluded his history of the work up to the year 1922 he added this text to it: 'And let the beauty of the LORD our God be upon us; and establish Thou the work of our hands upon us; yea, the work of our hands establish Thou it' (Psalm 90:17). Thirty-one years later the chairman of the Society spoke at the dedication of the new homes in the Midlands in 1953 and expressed the Society's strong commitment to 'the great doctrines of the Word of God which we know as the doctrines of Sovereign Grace. That is the solid Rock on which the Society was founded and has continued; and these doctrines are embodied in its Trust Deed.' He also expressed on that occasion his pleasure at seeing so many young people present, acknowledging that if the Society is to grow it must look to a younger generation for that growth.

It was, however, this strong emphasis on the doctrines of 'Sovereign Grace', coupled with the significant number of Strict Baptists who almost from the beginning had been substantial workers and supporters for the Society, that led the Aged Pilgrims' Friend Society to be seen by many as a charitable wing of the Strict Baptists. John Hazelton, the General Secretary for many years, was a Strict Baptist and had strong sympathies with the Gospel Standard denomination and had been invited to become pastor of their chapel in Gower Street, London. The Committee was increasingly heavily influenced by men of a similar denominational view, and an increasing number of residents also shared this background.

The tension between staying true to unchanging and eternal truths and yet being relevant to the challenges of a rapidly changing world had been present in the Society for many years as illustrated by the disquiet at the annual meeting in May 1878. There is little doubt that this held back the Society from some changes that were vitally necessary. Change began in 1947 when John Doggett joined the Committee. He became a leading barrister in government ministry and was frequently frustrated by the indecision of the Society's Committee. He was appointed chairman in 1977 and, whilst adhering firmly to the evangelical foundation of the Society, more Trustees were now appointed from the wider Christian community on the basis of their valued contribution rather than their church affiliation. He also pressed for an improvement of the existing homes and the building of many new ones right across the country to meet an increasing need.

It was inevitable that the ban, back in the 1930s, on residents owning a wireless would extend to the age of television. In fact, it was only in the 1980s, when the incongruity was recognised of resident staff being allowed a television whilst the pilgrims were not, that eventually relaxed this rule and allowed the residents themselves to decide. This change came only just before the Registered Homes Act of 1984 would doubtless have insisted on it anyway.

Spiralling costs and government intervention

Another significant change took place during the 1960s. Until then, without any funding from central or local government, the entire work of the Society was financed by the Christian public. In 1966 it became possible for residents to have part of their funding met by the local authorities, provided the home fulfilled all the requirements of the increasingly high standards demanded by the government—which the Society's homes did.

By 1967 the income of the Society was recorded as £98,000 of which £41,000 came from the state pension of the residents plus support from local authorities.

Inevitably, the high inflation of the late '70s and early '80s took its toll on the Society income. Inflation in 1973 was just over 9% jumping to 16% and then over 24% in the next two years respectively. This, together with fewer pensioners and more home residents, led to spiralling costs. In 1963 it cost on average £132 each to support the pensioners and residents; ten years later that average figure had risen to £762.[43]

The Registered Homes Act was soon supplemented by the Community Care Act of 1993 and the Care Standards Act of 2000. The Trustees who envisioned and built the first Aged Pilgrims' Friends Homes in 1834 could never have imagined the effect of government intervention one hundred and sixty years later.

The Community Care Act set out the understandable objective of encouraging the elderly to remain in their own home with suitable local authority support. This was not only a much cheaper option than residential care, but in general was far more acceptable to most elderly people. However, the effect was that increasingly, those who could no longer remain at home and therefore needed the security of a Pilgrim Home were older, more frail, and often with the first evidence of dementia. Caring for those with dementia in Pilgrim Homes, and providing resources to support carers in their own homes, has become a significant aspect of the Society's ministry in the 21st century. The slow but steady understanding of dementia is today a far cry from the situation in the 19th century when some of the residents were dismissed from their Pilgrim Home because of their unruly, erratic and sometimes aggressive behaviour—which we may not now find any easier to cope with, but at least we understand.

The Care Standards Act was a massive piece of legislation that went far beyond merely regulating homes. It introduced national minimum standards, in thirty-eight sections, and every home was to be inspected by the National Care Standards Commission (NCSC). The act covered every

---

43 The *Quarterly Record*, 1975, p. 50.

PILGRIMS'
FRIEND
SOCIETY

The Pilgrims' Magazine

Summer 2016

Photograph of Wales' River
Dee by artist/Dorothea Court
manager, Deryn van der Tang

CHRISTIANS
FOR OLDER
PEOPLE

- Unfurling new vision of Care despite financial storm

- Better care wings in with new Hummingbird approach at Framland

- Seniors changed teenagers lives by listening

*The cover of The Pilgrims' Magazine for the summer of 2016.
In full colour and a contemporary design it reflects the advance in
the Society's public image*

detail, including health and personal care, privacy and dignity, daily life and social activities, visiting, complaints and protection, environment, staffing, management and administration. All staff were committed to thorough training and the home manager, who is ultimately responsible for the daily care of the residents, faced a fine of £5,000 or six months imprisonment if found to be negligent and in breach of the standards required. It is little wonder that care homes across the country were soon in crisis with many closing simply because they could not absorb the high cost of meeting government regulations.

The *Quarterly Record* was in as much need of overhaul as many of the homes themselves. Its dull monochrome cover and bland design inside, gave a distinctly 'yesterday' feel. Colour was introduced in 1982 and with the steady improvement over the years, today *The Pilgrims' Magazine*, as it is now styled, is colourful, contemporary in its design, full of interesting articles, news and updates on its fifteen homes across the country.

One of the recommendations of a government inspection of the Society's homes in 1998 was that since 80% of the residents were women, they ought to be represented on the Committee. Two ladies were immediately appointed as Trustees. In 1985 Trevor Dennett, a professional accountant, was appointed as the Society's Financial Secretary and this radically improved the financial arrangements and economies of the whole Society. The Aged Pilgrims' Friend Society was slowly emerging 'from the shadow of aversion to change'. The newly created position of Chief Executive was filled by Trevor Dennett in 1992 and subsequently by Peter Tervet. By now the number of staff employed by the headquarters in Tower Bridge Road, London had increased to manage the ever-widening scope of the Society's work and the increasing government legislation regulating the care of the elderly.

A change of name

As far back as 1912 one speaker had commented on what he considered 'the quaint spirituality' of the Society's name. He reflected that, at the time of the Society's foundation, it was perfectly acceptable and could have been a lot worse, suggesting that 'The Society for the Relief of the Indigent and Pious Poor' might well have been chosen.[44]

Seventy years later the title was a negative barrier to staff appointments and recommending the work to the Christian public. By 1987 there were only six pensioners, yet almost 400 residents in thirteen homes. The high point of 1,684 pensioners in 1909 had steadily declined. The urgent need for the Society was now for residential homes rather than pensions.

By 1989 the Society adopted a new name of 'Pilgrim Homes'. A further change was made in 2010 when the wider work of the Society was recognised in the name 'Pilgrims' Friend Society'.

The latter half of the 20th century saw a significant increase in the number of homes, and by the end of the first decade of the 21st century fifteen homes could offer between them a range of care including: independent living, residential care, retirement living, extra care housing, dementia care and respite care.

The new logo and change of name adopted in 1989

---

44 The *Quarterly Record*, 1912, p. 75.

*The dedicated and highly trained staff are the greatest asset for the
ministry of Pilgrim Homes*

HOUSING
DESIGN
AWARDS
HAPPI WINNER
2012

PILGRIMS'
FRIEND
SOCIETY

Pilgrim Gardens is
'Best Housing Project
of 2014'

Our occupants are precious to God
and to us. They deserve the best
building, the best ethos, the best
support, and the best service

The award-winning Evington complex in Leicestershire opened in 2014

8. Facing the future

As the Society moved into its third century in 2007 the Trustees reflected on the original purposes and motivations of the Society. The considerable expertise that it had developed in Christian care for older people led them to believe that this could be used to help churches and families in their own care of the elderly.

To mark the bi-centenary of the work, the Society hosted a conference in London with other interested organisations under the title: The World, the Church and Older People. The day conference was planned for Wednesday 21 November 2007 and a modest number was expected. In the event over 400 registered. The keynote ministry from Psalm 92:14 'They will still bear fruit in old age...', together with the enthusiasm of all who attended the day of seminars, and the prompting of friends, led the Trustees to believe that older pilgrims in every town and city in the country might benefit from the Society's work. This could be through a home where one existed and elsewhere by churches and families using the Society's resources and training.

Independent nursing and residential care homes continued to face the threat of increasing regulation and financial pressures. The development of the Society's work outside of the homes was put on pause partly because other Christian run care homes were calling on the Society for help and advice, and partly because of the need to get their own legal structure in order in the light of changes in government regulations.

In 2010, the governance of the Society was updated with a corporate trustee established (Pilgrims' Friend Society) in line with recommended practice for a charity of such a size and complexity. Pilgrims' Friend Society became something close to the lead charity for the group; consultation processes were established to streamline what could otherwise have become unwieldy membership arrangements.

Chapter 8

A new direction

At the same time, the Trustees responded positively to requests from other Christian run care homes that were finding it increasingly difficult to maintain their work. This meant that, in addition to their traditional Pilgrim Homes, the Trustees agreed to run a range of other homes that provided Christian support in a Christian environment; these homes were open to people who wanted to live in a Christian environment and were prepared to acknowledge the Society's basis of faith, yet who could not necessarily provide a testimony of conversion. These were incorporated together into a separate charity called 'Pilgrim Havens'. The homes that still required a validated testimony of Christian conversion were held under the original 1807 charity 'Pilgrim Homes'.

These changes allowed the Society to support the running of the Ernest Luff home and the Olive Luff home in Walton-on-the-Naze and the Anna Victoria nursing home. Subsequently, the Society acquired additional homes managed in a similar manner: Emmaus House in Harrogate; Bethany Christian Home in Plymouth and Florence House in Peterborough.

The assimilation of these homes was not always straightforward because, although the Society was better resourced to manage the homes, it was not immune from the issues confronting the older premises in both these and their own homes. Despite its best endeavours, the Society was forced to close some homes whilst at the same time building new ones. The homes closed included the Wellesborough Home, Anna Victoria Nursing Home, and a major reconfiguration of the care available on the Ernest Luff site which began in 2015.

Following a significant investment in Royd Court—a new extra care housing scheme built in Mirfield, West Yorkshire—the Society invested in a major refurbishment of the Evington nursing home. An award-winning development of 31 independent living housing units, Pilgrim Gardens, replaced the bungalows built in 1954 and by now rather dated. Described as 'a home for life', this beautiful complex was formally opened on Saturday 6 September 2014 under the banner: 'Christians supporting older people and shaping the issues that affect them.'[45]

By 2015 the dust had settled on these changes and the recruitment of Stephen Hammersley CBE as the Chief Executive Officer of the Pilgrims' Friend Society marked the point at which the Trustees wanted to press ahead on two key fronts: developing and investing in Christian care through its homes and supporting increasing numbers of churches that were needing help to care for their elderly in the community. There can be no doubt that the Aged Pilgrims' Friend Society had moved decidedly and determinedly into a new future, and not simply by a change of name. From his background as head of marketing in a major UK bank, via significant responsibilities in Christian and other charities, the new CEO brought substantial expertise to Pilgrims' Friend Society as it moved forward in the 21st century.

Building on everything that has gone in the past—both the strong evangelical base and the equally strong commitment to the elderly Christians in our society—it is to the credit of the Trustees that a two-hundred-year old charity was able to adapt to the huge changes of recent decades in order to better fulfil its mission. However, these changes were no less significant than those facing the Trustees who, years earlier, decided that housing provision was needed to go alongside pension provision, and those who recognised the increasing irrelevancy and unaffordability of the pensions that had been the original purpose of the mission.

Studies on the subject of ageing in our population present a challenging picture for the government, and also for Christians who acknowledge their responsibility to contribute to the well-being not only of the 'aged pilgrims' but to society as a whole.

---

45 The complex was the winner of the 2014 HAPPI award from the Housing our Ageing Population Panel for Innovation (HAPPI).

A Visitor and elderly Pilgrims today

The elderly are growing older

The population of the UK is ageing. There are more than 10.3 million people aged 65 and over in the UK (that is approximately 18% of the total population) and the projection is that this will rise to 12.7 million in 2018 and is expected to reach 16.9 million by 2035.[46] That last figure is equivalent to the entire population of the Netherlands in 2016!

Interestingly, this growth of the older age groups has not happened equally for both sexes. Faster improvements in mortality rates for men mean that the number of men aged 75 and over has increased by 149% since mid-1974 while the number of women in that age group has grown only by 61%. This progress in the life expectancy of men is due partly to a reduction in smoking, significant advances in cardiovascular treatment, and in healthier lifestyles.[47]

Not only is the population ageing, but there has been progressive ageing of the older population. Most striking has been the increase in the number and proportion of the 'oldest old'. In 1984, 19% of the population aged 65 and over were in their 80s and 2% were aged 90 and over. By 2014, this had risen to 22% and 5% respectively.[48]

This increase in longevity is not expected to halt either. One research study has gone so far as to assume that the 'march of human life expectancy will continue unchecked, and that there will not come a point in the foreseeable future where humans will reach an age at which further increases in life expectancy is beyond the physiological capacity of the ageing body and mind'.[49] In brief, this means that with the steady advances in medical care generally, and of the elderly in particular, we have little idea how long it is physically possible for anyone to live—an interesting insight into the longevity of early biblical characters!

46 House of Commons Library: Population Ageing Statistics, 10 February 2012.
47 Office for National Statistics, 25 June 2015.
48 Office for National Statistics, 30 September 2015.
49 On line: 'Estimating the future healthcare costs of an aging population in the UK: expansion of morbidity and the need for preventative care', Michael Caley, Specialist Registrar in Public Health and Khesh Sidhu, Consultant in Public Health Medicine. However, more recently some researches consider 115 years as being the optimum possible age.

Chapter 8

The economic value of the elderly

However, although it is a given that there is a significant cost factor involved in an ageing population—the number of older people with care-needs is expected to rise by more than 60% in the next 20 years—the negative approach to the economic 'burden' of the elderly is far too one-sided. After deduction of the costs of pensions, welfare and health care, the Women's Royal Voluntary Service have estimated that the over-65s make a net contribution to the UK economy of £40 billion through tax payments, spending power, donations to charities and volunteering.

In a similar study, The King's Fund has drawn attention to the economic value of an ageing population. Financially older people contribute significantly to society. Many continue in full or part-time work well beyond the age of 65.[50] They have a spending power of £76 billion which is expected to rise to £127 billion by 2030, a growth of 68%. The many older people who undertake voluntary charitable work, including family care, has a hidden value estimated to be in the region of £10 billion a year. In addition, they are known to be more generous in their donations to charitable work, also estimated to be in the region of £10 billion a year. The King's Fund concludes that if people can stay healthy for longer, they will remain valued and engaged members of society.

None of these conclusions take into account the wisdom, advice, experience and encouragement that many elderly members give back to society and on which no monetary value could ever be placed.

The spiritual and pastoral value of elderly Pilgrims

Psalm 92:14 'The righteous ... will still bear fruit in old age.'

Throughout its history over more than two hundred years, the Pilgrims' Friend Society has consistently referred to the value of elderly Christians. This was rarely recognised by many of the churches to which they had

---

50 The Office for National Statistics estimates that in 2010, of those aged 65 and over 2.7% (270,000) worked full-time and 6.1% (600,000) worked part-time.

been attached throughout their life and it is a sad comment to read of those who had few people to visit them and no one to take them to their chapel or church; they lived alone and frail in their meagre lodgings. This is where the Society made such a huge difference to the lives of the many thousands to whom they paid a small pension. Equally important as the pension were the regular visits to read the Scriptures, pray and encourage the elderly Pilgrims. When the homes were opened, hundreds more were able to enjoy the closing years of their life in the context of Christian care and understanding.

However, even today the spiritual value of Pilgrims is rarely appreciated. Where the churches do care for the elderly members of their congregation, it is often thought of as how we can 'look after them'. Few churches think imaginatively how elderly Pilgrims may continue to be a rich source of support, wisdom and blessing to the Christian community.

As long ago as 1907 the *Quarterly Record* commented, 'It would do our young pilgrims good, as part of a sound Christian education, if they would now and then go and see old pilgrims, and hear them bear their testimony for Jesus.'[51] Perhaps the truth of that needs reiterating today. It is generally only the testimony of those being baptised, or young people engaged in some exciting Christian service, or those involved in daily life in the world, that is heard by our congregations. We overlook the value of hearing the life story of an elderly Christian who has proved the grace of God through countless encouragements, discouragements, joys and tragedies in a long life of eighty or ninety years or more. There can be few more powerful testimonies to the keeping power of God and the reality of Christian faith than that. Perhaps there needs to be a much greater link between the youth leaders and the elderly in our churches.

The increasing number of elderly Pilgrims in our churches could, with thoughtful planning, be formed into an effective army of prayer warriors for every aspect of the life of the church. For this, they need to be kept regularly informed, and so brought into the very heart of the life of the church. This needs to be seen, not as a postscript to church life just to keep

---

51 John E Hazelton, *"Inasmuch": A History of the Aged Pilgrims' Friend Society 1807–1907.*

the elderly occupied, but as a vital ministry within the life of the fellowship. Keeping the elderly prayer warriors informed should be every bit as well organised and highly prioritised as any other aspect of church work.

Church leaders may well find it helpful to consult some elderly members on matters relating to church life and history. This does not mean that they are expected to veto or run the church, but the wisdom, insights and experience of many older members can sometimes save younger leaders from making unnecessary mistakes. Unfortunately, it is often assumed that because elderly members come from a different generation they must be 'out of touch' with the present world. In reality they have lived through, and therefore are familiar with, vast changes; age does not always mean aversion to change or ignorance of its value.

Pilgrim Homes staff are dedicated and aware of the need for constant improvement in today's highly regulated care environment. In-service training is a high priority for Pilgrims' Friend Society

Challenges for the future

Of course, there will inevitably come a time in the life of the growing older elderly when they may not be able to contribute because of their loss of memory or mind, and this presents new challenges. Even for those who are cared for in their own home there are particular issues to be faced. The ministry of the Pilgrims' Friend Society is always alert to the need to adapt to changing situations and challenges.

- *The challenge of cost.* One of the most media publicised issues in this context confronting the 21st century society is the high cost of caring for the very frail elderly. Successive governments will be unable to afford the luxury of adequate care in purpose-built homes with highly motivated staff; a greater expectation will fall to the voluntary sector. Similarly, smaller independent homes will find it increasingly difficult to remain viable. Whatever the value of maintaining the elderly in their own home, there will be a growing need for residential accommodation. With governments less inclined to pay for such costs, the responsibility will fall upon supporting Christians and churches to build and maintain such homes. The church must rise to this challenge, and Pilgrims' Friend Society can act as a significant catalyst for this.

- *The challenge of providing dedicated staff* who are not only well trained but committed with a Christian heart and with Christian values to a loving and dignified care of the elderly, whether they are Christians or not. The tragic record in recent years of cruelty in many state and private care homes illustrates the difficulty of recruiting staff of the highest calibre. This has become critical in recent years and for this reason many Christian residential homes are part staffed by those who do not share the same full commitment to Christ. This will never be resolved unless churches encourage their young people to enter this field of ministry as a career of dignity, value and respect. It may not appear as exciting as travelling overseas to care for those in need, and currently it does not capture the imagination of our congregations, but it is every bit as important and equally valuable for the Kingdom of God.

- *The challenge of dementia and Alzheimer's care.* Unless or until an effective way is found of curing or delaying the onset of the distressing loss of mental power in the very elderly, there will be an ever-increasing need to understand both the patients and especially those who care for them. Carers, many of whom are themselves old, often reach the point where they need those they can trust to help in the heavy burden of care and respite. No community is better equipped to support in this way than the Christian churches. The task of caring for carers both at home and in Pilgrim Homes is vital, and few organisations are better equipped to advise, counsel, and care than Pilgrims' Friend Society. It already produces helpful literature and conferences covering these areas.

- *The challenge of ensuring meaningful lifestyles for the elderly.* The economic and spiritual value of elderly Pilgrims has already been referred to, but even for those who are no longer able to make an obvious contribution to the work of the Kingdom, there must be imaginative ways of encouraging them to experience more in life than vacantly sitting day after day doing nothing.

- *The challenge of encouraging churches to be significantly involved in the life of the elderly in general and the work of Pilgrims' Friend Society in particular.* Many churches simply overlook the elderly when they are no longer sitting in church, or even when they are. For those who have little choice but to enter a residential home, they are frequently lost from the fellowship of all but a few faithful visitors.

- *The challenge of involving younger people in the support of the elderly.* In 1922 a specific appeal was made to young people to maintain the work that was commenced by young people 115 years earlier: 'We look to you, thank God that an increasing number of your own generation are engaged in this service.'[52] Those who commenced the work in 1807 were probably in their late 20s and early 30s. However, it is that very age-group today that is generally so little involved in caring for the elderly.

---

52 John E Hazelton, *"Inasmuch": A History of the Aged Pilgrims' Friend Society 1807–1922* (London: C J Farncombe & Sons, 1922), pp. 158-159.

A group of young disciples from an evangelical church in London, in July 1990, visiting to sing for a terminally ill member of their church

- *The challenge of interesting our children in the care of the elderly.* A report in 1910 commented that three children had been made Life Subscribers by the payment of £10.10 shillings and added, 'It would delight the Board to be permitted to add to this list, with the hope that the youthful donors may, in the course of years, take an active, intelligent, and spiritual interest in the Society.' Perhaps it should be part of every children's and youth leader's programme to introduce the younger lives in their care to older Pilgrims,

A young child chatting to Millie at Shottermill House on her 100th birthday in May 2011

so that they may find ways of caring for and learning from the mature experience of Pilgrims who have been close friends of God for many years.

• *The challenge of bringing the needs of our elderly much higher on the agenda of church leaders.* At the dedication of the new Pilgrim homes in the Midlands in 1953 the chairman of the Society expressed pleasure at seeing so many young people present, acknowledging that if the Society is to grow it must look to a younger generation for that growth. Sadly, young people are rarely seen at such meetings today and this is because few church leaders are themselves there and they do not expect, or encourage, young people to attend.

• *The challenge of government intervention.* With increasing ideological regulations from central government ministers and the imposition of their invented 'British values', there is likely to be more political intrusion into the way Christian homes are run. This will prove a challenge to all evangelical ministries.

• *The challenge of confronting society's shifting and falling standards.* A society driven by an evolutionary philosophy will inevitably determine the value of the individual by its economic contribution. The growing lobby for personal choice in abortion and euthanasia is driven by the same philosophy. This is contrary to the Christian ethos of seeing everyone as created in the image and likeness of God, and therefore all life as valuable from conception to the grave. Christian congregations, and especially the children and young people, need to be constantly reminded that the old and frail person suffering from dementia still has the dignity of being created in the image of God.

• *The challenge of growing old.* Christians must be taught how to grow old with dignity, purpose and grace. The challenges facing those who are more frail and less active are different, but no less real, than those facing our young people and young families. The Scriptures address every stage of life with spiritual and practical instruction; it is as essential that Pilgrims are prepared for growing old as much as teens are equipped for entering higher education and the world of work.

With the passing of more than two centuries, the work of Pilgrims' Friend Society is as necessary today as ever. Across the United Kingdom, standards of living, expectations of longevity, medical care, governmental regulations and interference, society's secular philosophy, church life and much besides, bear little resemblance to the London of 1807. However, a constant in every generation since the creation of mankind has been the fact of growing old, and with it increasing frailty and dependence. Certainly, a mark of a civilised society is the way it cares for the elderly. In the light of the many encouragements from Scripture, it is equally a mark of the healthy Christian church.

Pilgrims' Friend Society is vigorously confronting the challenges of the 21st century and is always ready to assist those caring for the elderly and to adjust to the changing circumstances of our times.

If the record is correct, the Aged Pilgrims' Friend Society was inspired by a sermon preached by John Hyatt on Wednesday evening 5 August 1807 from Job 29:12,13

'Because I delivered the poor that cried, and the fatherless, and him that had none to help him. The blessing of him that was ready to perish came upon me: and I caused the widow's heart to sing for joy.'

Nothing has changed in the commitment of the Pilgrims' Friend Society.

The original articles of the Aged Pilgrims' Friends Society

(A facsimile of this page is on page 22)

Wednesday, September 2 1807

At a meeting of a considerable number of friends to the intended institution for the relief of the aged and infirm christian poor in destitute circumstances, held this evening by adjournment. The following rules were agreed upon. First the title page.

The
Aged Pilgrims Friend
Society
Instituted August 12th 1807
For the Relief of
The Aged and Infirm
Christian Poor
at
No 13 Great Peartree Street
Goswell Street

We know that we have passed from death unto life because we love the brethren   1 John 3.14.

Now concerning the collection for the saints as I have given order to the churches of Galatia, even so do ye 1 Cor.16.1
London
Printed by
1807

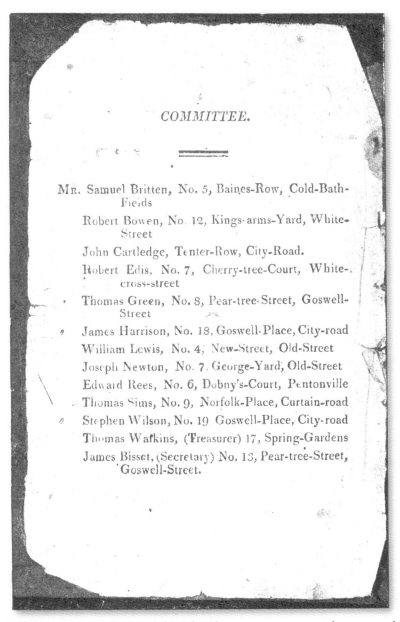

Following the original articles, the above persons were chosen on the committee for the first year

Resolved unanimously

That the address already circulated be printed with the articles as the introduction.

Resolved unanimously

1. That the society now formed is for the purpose of granting annuities of five guineas each during life unto such aged and infirm persons as are of the household of faith and is denominated The Aged Pilgrims Friend Society.

2. That for this purpose subscriptions be entered into (either monthly or quarterly or annual) from six pence per month upwards. The first payment to be made upon entrance (also occasional donations of any amount). A person making a donation of ten guineas at one time to be considered a governor for life.

3. That a committee not exceeding thirteen nor less than five be annually chosen at the General meeting in December to receive subscriptions, donations and legacies and transact the other business of the society. Who shall meet the last Monday in every month at eight o'clock in the evening at No 13 Great Peartree Street, Goswell Street, any three of whom with the treasurer and secretary shall have power to act. If any member of the committee dies or leaves the society during the year, and it should be found necessary to fill up the vacancy, a general meeting of the society shall be summoned (at such time and place shall be agreed upon) for that purpose.

4. That a treasurer and secretary shall be chosen annually who shall constitute part of the committee and with the other members give their services gratuitously to the society.

5. That the cases elected on the society shall be visited by each member of the committee in rotation monthly and the report made at the ensuing monthly meetings, if any member who has a case should be unable to visit it during his month he shall get another member of the committee to visit it for him that month, in order that no case may on any account be neglected.

6. That as this Society is formed exclusively for the relief of the aged and infirm children of God (of both sexes) in necessitous circumstances, such a persons only as belong to Christian churches or who can give satisfactory evidence of being members of the mystical body of Christ of the age of sixty and upwards and whose income does not exceed five shillings per week can be relieved by this society.

7. That person is thus qualified being recommended by a subscriber according to the articles, stating the full particulars of the person's qualification in writing shall upon the motion of any one or more of the committee have their names and place of abode entered on the case list, and elected by ballot by the committee at the monthly meetings when the fund will admit.

8. That the number of persons thus elected shall receive from the society the sum of five guineas per annum (in weekly payments or otherwise at the discretion of the committee) during life or so long as they shall continue objects according to the rules exclusive of any gifts the society may at any time have to make in books, wearing apparel etc

9. That the visitors shall ask the persons visited such questions as they shall think necessary to satisfy their minds that they are proper objects, and report the same the meeting night following in order to prevent as much as possible the society being imposed upon by false representations.

10. That if it shall afterward appear that any person has been elected contrary to the design of this institution as described in the sixth article, the circumstances of the case shall be fully enquired into and laid before the committee at the following meeting night after it is discovered and if the majority of the members then present shall declare by vote that the person ought not to have been elected, the case shall be discontinued and the name of the person struck off the books of the society.

11. That a General meeting of the society be held twice in every year (namely the last week in June and December) at such time and place as shall be agreed upon by the committee at the previous monthly meeting. The

subscribers to be summoned to attend, a minister requested to give an exhortation, and a collection made, and as often as the committee shall think it necessary, a sermon shall be preached at some established place of public worship for the benefits of the institution.

12. That any person whose subscription amounts to ten and six pence per annum or two persons subscribing six pence per month each be at liberty to recommend one case to the committee, subscribers of one guinea two cases and so on in proportion, but those who have cases relieved by the society shall not recommend any other while they are on the books and no recommendation can be attended to from any subscriber who has not subscribed six months and who subscription is not paid up previous to the recommendation.

13. That when the fund of this society shall amount to ten guineas as many cases shall be elected as the annual amount of subscriptions at that time will pay annuities. The number to be increased as often as the additional amount of subscriptions within the year shall amount to one years annuity.

14. That if any persons who may be relieved by this society should be found at any time living in any known sin it shall be reported to the committee by the person who discovers it, two of the members shall then be appointed to see the offending party and warn them of their error. If they will not hear them, they shall be summoned before the committee who shall faithfully admonish them, but if the offence is still continued, the party shall be struck off the books.

15. That every person who shall be elected a member of the committee shall give his experience at the time of election and answer such questions as shall be put to him by the committee in order that no person may be appointed to visit the Lord's family but such as are of the household of faith and whose known principles are strictly consistent with the word of God.

16. That books of accounts be kept of all monies received and paid, the names and places of abode of each person relieved and by whom

recommended, also minutes of the proceedings of the society from time to time, which books may be examined by any subscriber as often as required.

17. That if any subscriber should have anything to propose which cannot be determined by these articles it shall be stated to the committee at their monthly meeting, and if necessary a special meeting of them shall be summoned to take the proposition into consideration which shall be decided by a majority of the committee then present.

18. That all meetings of the committee and the society begin and end with prayer. Such persons as may be disposed to aid this important institution by subscriptions or donations are requested to give their names and place of abode to the secretary or any member of the committee.

NB. Donations of Bibles and Testaments will be thankfully received and as many of the dear Old Pilgrims are found almost naked, the committee will gladly receive new or old wearing apparel and pledge themselves to distribute it unto those they judge most in want.

The following form of bequest is recommended unto those who may be desirous of aiding this institution by legacy.

I give and bequeath unto the treasurer for the time being of the Aged Pilgrims Friend Society instituted August 12 1807 for the purpose of granting annuities of five guineas each unto the aged and infirm Christian poor whose committee meet at no 13 Great Peartree Street, Goswell Street the sum of .... to be paid out of my personal estate within .... months after my decease, the treasurer's receipt shall be taken and deemed a sufficient discharge for the same.

[These articles were read and confirmed by the committee on Monday September 7th 1807 and it was resolved immediately to print 250 copies. They were amended in June 1810, new rules were added in June 1825 which brought the number to 32 and they were revised again in 1832.]

A hymn written by Dr Horatius Bonar for the Aged Pilgrims' Friend Society in September 1884

But Thou Art Rich
Rev.ii.9

"I know thy poverty; but thou art rich,
For all I have is thine, —
My heaven, My glory, and My throne!
Canst thou, My child, repine?

I know thy poverty; but thou art rich,
For I Myself am Thine,
And thou, for whom I gave My life,
Yes, thou thyself, art Mine!

Think'st thou I could not give the earthly gold,
From royal stores above?
Is My eternal fullness drained,
Or have I ceased to love?

'Twas better that thou should'st be poor on earth,
And thus I chose thy lot.
Canst thou misdoubt a love like Mine,
Or deem thyself forgot?

This passing world is poor, but thou art rich!
'Tis rich, but thou art poor.
Thy poverty is but a day;
Thy riches evermore.

I know thy poverty; but not the less
Art thou, My chosen one.
Heir of eternal riches, think
How soon there comes the throne!

All things are thine, beloved; life or death,
Or wealth or poverty.
The blood of Him who died, and rose,
Has brought them all for thee.

Things present or to come — thy Father's house,
With all its bright abodes!
Claim thou thy heritage, for thou art Christ's,
And Christ is God's.

The things that I have never seen, nor ear
Hath heard, are all in sight.
The day of gladness comes apace,
Tears are but for a night."

Horatius Bonar
September 1884

Appendix C

The record of Pilgrim Friends' Society Homes (PFS) and Havens (H)

We are thankful to God for those homes that are currently providing care and support to older Christians.

Home	Starting date as a Pilgrim Friends' Society home
Brighton Home, Brighton, East Sussex (PFS)	October 1879
Evington Home, Evington, Leicestershire (PFS)	April 1954
Pilgrim Gardens, Evington, Leicestershire (PFS)	September 2014
Milward House, Tunbridge Wells, Kent (PFS)	May 1972
Leonora Home, Chippenham, Wiltshire (PFS)	October 1974
Finborough Court, Stowmarket, Suffolk (PFS)	May 1983
Framland, Wantage, Oxfordshire (PFS)	April 1986
Shottermill House, Haslemere, Surrey (PFS)	June 1990
Royd Court, Mirfield, West Yorkshire (PFS)	December 2006
Dorothea Court, Bedford, Bedfordshire (PFS)	November 2008
Luff House, Walton-on-the-Naze, Essex (H)	April 2010
Redbourn Missionary Housing, Hertfordshire (PFS)	April 2010
Bethany Christian Home, Plymouth, Devon (H)	July 2011
Florence House, Peterborough, Cambridgeshire (H)	April 2012
Emmaus House, Harrogate, North Yorkshire (H)	April 2012

A staff member and resident at Leonora home in Chippenham

130 When evangelicals care

We also thankful to God for the principal PFS homes that provided care to so many elderly Christians until the home reached a point where its ongoing services could not be sustained.

Home	Date of opening and closure
Camberwell, London	1838 – 1991
Hornsey Rise, London	1871 – 1973
Stamford Hill, London	1883 – 1986
Gerrards Cross, Buckinghamshire	1888 – 1973
Winchester, Hampshire	1899 – 1999
Kirkman Home, Tunbridge Wells, Kent	1925 – 1990
Hollington, Hastings, East Sussex	1966 – 1975
The Ruth Cowell Home, Bristol	1968 – 2004
The Hazleton Home, St Leonards-on-Sea, East Sussex	1973 – 1991
Hornsey Rise Memorial Home, Wellsborough, Warwickshire	1973 – 2013
The Gables, Southport, Merseyside	1983 – 2001
Brackloon, Seaham, Durham	1997 – 2001
Anna Victoria Nursing Home, Frinton-on-Sea	2011 – 2013

Residents, staff and visitors at Emmaus House in April 2014